The Aquarian Sun Sign Guides

SCORPIO

Bernard Fitzwalter has been interested in astrology since he was about six, when he played King Herod's astrologer in his primary school nativity play. For the past six years he has been teaching astrology for the Marylebone-Paddington Institute, and for seven years he has had a regular column in OVER 21 magazine. In 1984 he appeared in the first series of Anglia Television's *Zodiac Game*, which prompted the *Daily Mirror* to say that he was 'enough to give astrology a good name'.

AQUARIAN SUN SIGN GUIDES

SCORPIO

23 OCTOBER – 21 NOVEMBER

Bernard Fitzwalter

Cover illustration by Steinar Lund
Cover typography by Steven Lee

THE AQUARIAN PRESS
Wellingborough, Northamptonshire

First published 1987

© BERNARD FITZWALTER 1987

British Library Cataloguing in Publication Data

Fitzwalter, Bernard
Scorpio.—(The Aquarian sun sign guides)
1. Zodiac
I. Title
133.5'4   BF1728.A2

ISBN 0-85030-582-9

*The Aquarian Press is part of the
Thorsons Publishing Group*

Printed and bound in Great Britain

Contents

PART 4: SCORPIO TRIVIA

Introduction

This book has been written to help you find out a little about astrology and a lot about yourself. It explains, for the first time, the motives and aims that guide your actions and make you do things the way you do; what it does not do is give you a list of 'typical Scorpio' things to see if you recognize any of them. You are not likely to be typical anything: you are unique. What you *do* have in common with others who have birthdays at about the same time as you is a way of using your energy, a way of thinking, a set of motives and beliefs which seem to make sense to you, and which other people, those of the other eleven signs, obviously do not have. This book shows you those motives and beliefs, and shows you how they fit in with those of the other eleven signs. The zodiac is like a jigsaw: all the pieces have to be there for the whole picture to emerge.

This book also sets out to answer some very simple questions which are often asked but seldom answered. Questions like 'Why does the zodiac have twelve signs?' and 'What does being a Scorpio actually mean?' as well as 'Why are Scorpios supposed to be intense? Why can't they be easygoing instead? and why don't all the people of the same star sign look the same?'

The reason that these questions are seldom answered is because all too many astrologers don't know the rudiments of astrological theory, and what they do know they don't tell, because they think it is too difficult for the man in the street to understand. This is obvious nonsense: astrology was devised for and by people who did not normally read or write as much as we do, nor did they all have PhDs or the equivalent. The man in the street is quite capable of understanding anything provided that it is shown simply and clearly, from first principles upwards, and provided he has sufficient interest. Buying this book is evidence enough of your interest, and I hope that the explanations are simple enough and clear enough for you. If they are not, it is my fault, and not that of astrology.

How to Use this Book

The book is in four parts. It is best to read them in sequence, but if you have neither time nor patience, then they each work individually. Part 2 does not assume that you have read Part 1, though it helps. Part 3 makes a lot more sense if you have already read Parts 1 and 2, but it isn't mandatory. Part 4, although just as firmly based on astrological principles as the other three, is deliberately intended as light relief.

The first part of the book deals with the theory behind the zodiac; it sets out the principles of astrology and enables you to see why Scorpio is assigned the qualities it has, how the ruling planet system works, and what all the other signs are like in terms of motivation, so you can compare them to your own. There is a short and effective method given for assessing the aims and motives of other people. When you read Part 3 you will need to know a bit about the other signs, as you will be finding out that you have more to you than just the Scorpio part you knew about.

The second part describes the essential Scorpio. It shows you how there are different sorts of Scorpios according to where your birthday falls in the month, and shows how Scorpio energy is used differently in the Scorpio as a child, adult, and parent.

Since you spend the greatest part of your life in dealing with other individuals, the way Scorpio deals with relationships is treated in some detail. This is the largest section of the book.

The third part shows you a different kind of zodiac, and enables you to go into your own life in much greater detail. It isn't complicated, but you do need to think. It crosses the border between the kind of astrology you get in the magazines, and the sort of thing a real astrologer does. There's no reason why you can't do it yourself because, after all, you know yourself best.

The fourth part shows you the surface of being a Scorpio, and how the zodiacal energy comes out in your clothes, your home, even your favourite food. The final item of this part actually explains the mechanics of being lucky, which you probably thought was impossible.

I hope that when you finish reading you will have a clearer view of yourself, and maybe like yourself a little more. Don't put the book away and forget about it; read it again in a few months' time—you will be surprised at what new thoughts about yourself it prompts you to form!

Note

Throughout this book, the pronouns 'he', 'him', and 'his' have been used to describe both male and female. Everything which applies to a male Scorpio applies to a female Scorpio as well. There are two reasons why I have not bothered to make the distinction: firstly, to avoid long-windedness; secondly, because astrologically there is no need. It is not possible to tell from a horoscope whether the person to whom it relates is male or female, because to astrology they are both living individuals full of potential.

BERNARD FITZWALTER

Part 1

How the Zodiac Works

1. The Meaning of the Zodiac

Two Times Two is Four; Four Times Three is Twelve

It is no accident that there are twelve signs in the zodiac, although there are a great many people who reckon themselves to be well versed in astrology who do not know the reasons why, and cannot remember ever having given thought to the principles behind the circle of twelve.

The theory is quite simple, and once you are familiar with it, it will enable you to see the motivation behind all the other signs as well as your own. What's more, you only have to learn nine words to do it. That's quite some trick—being able to understand what anybody else you will ever meet is trying to do, with nine words.

It works like this.

The zodiac is divided into twelve signs, as you know. Each of the twelve represents a stage in the life cycle of solar energy as it is embodied in the life of mankind here on our planet. There are tides in this energy; sometimes it flows one way, sometimes another, like the tides of the ocean. Sometimes it is held static, in the form of an object, and sometimes it is released when that object is broken down after a period of time. The twelve signs show all these processes, both physical and spiritual, in their interwoven pattern.

Six signs are used to show the flowing tide, so to speak, and six for the ebbing tide. Aries, Gemini, Leo, Libra, Sagittarius, and Aquarius are the 'flowing' group, and the others form the second group. You will notice at once that the signs alternate, one with the other, around the zodiac, so that the movement is maintained, and there is never a concentration of one sort of energy in one place. People whose Sun sign is in the first group tend to radiate their energies outwards from themselves. They are the ones who like to make the first move, like to be the ones to take command of a situation, like to put something of themselves into whatever they are doing. They don't feel right standing on the sidelines; they are the original have-a-go types. Energy comes out of them and is radiated towards other people, in the same way as the Sun's energy is radiated out to the rest of the solar system.

The people in the other signs are the opposite to that, as you would expect. They collect all the energy from the first group, keeping it for themselves and making sure none is wasted. They absorb things from a situation or from a personal contact, rather than contributing to it. They prefer to watch and learn rather than make the first move. They correspond to the Moon, which collects and reflects the energy of the Sun. One group puts energy out, one group takes it back in. The sum total of energy in the universe remains constant, and the two halves of the zodiac gently move to and fro with the tide of the energies.

This energy applies both to the real and concrete world of objects, as well as to the intangible world of thoughts inside our heads.

A distinction has to be made, then, between the real world and the intangible world. If this is done, we have four kinds of energy: outgoing and collecting, physical and mental. These four kinds of energy have been recognized for a long time, and were given names to describe the way they work more than two thousand years ago. These are the elements. All the energy in the cosmos can be described in the terms of these four: Fire, Earth, Air, Water.

Fire is used to describe that outgoing energy which applies to the real and physical world. There are three signs given to it: Aries, Leo, and Sagittarius. People with the Sun in any of these

igns find themselves with the energy to get things going. They
are at their best when making a personal contribution to a
situation, and they expect to see some tangible results for their
efforts. They are sensitive to the emotional content of anything,
but that is not their prime concern, and so they tend to let it look
after itself while they busy themselves with the actual matter in
hand. Wherever you meet Fire energy in action, it will be shown
as an individual whose personal warmth and enthusiasm are
having a direct effect on his surroundings.

Earth is used to describe the real and physical world where the
energies are being collected and stored, sometimes in the form
of material or wealth. The three signs given to the element are
Taurus, Virgo, and Capricorn. Where Fire energy in people
makes them want to move things, Earth energy makes them want
to hold things and stop them moving. The idea of touching and
holding, and so that of possession, is important to these people,
and you can usually see it at work in the way they behave
towards their own possessions. The idea is to keep things stable,
and to hold energy stored for some future time when it will be
released. Earth Sun people work to ensure that wherever they are
is secure and unlikely to change; if possible they would like the
strength and wealth of their situation to increase, and will work
towards that goal. Wherever you meet Earth energy in action,
there will be more work being done than idle chat, and there will
be a resistance to any kind of new idea. There will be money
being made, and accumulated. The idea of putting down roots
and bearing fruit may be a useful one to keep in mind when
trying to understand the way this energy functions.

Air is used to describe outgoing mental energies; put more
simply, this is communication. Here the ideas are formed in the
mind of the individual, and put out in the hope that they can
influence and meet the ideas of another individual; this is
communication, in an abstract sense. Gemini, Libra, and
Aquarius are all Air signs, and people with the Sun in those signs
are very much concerned with communicating their energies to
others. Whether anything gets done as a result of all the
conversation is not actually important; if there is to be a

concrete result, then that is the province of Fire or Earth energies. Here the emphasis is on shaping the concept, not the reality. There is an affinity with Fire energies, because both of them are outgoing, but other than that they do not cross over into each other's territory. Wherever you meet Air energy in action, there is a lot of talk, and new ideas are thrown up constantly, but there is no real or tangible result, no real product, and no emotional involvement; were there to be emotional content, the energies would be watery ones.

Water is the collection of mental energies. It is the response to communication or action. It absorbs and dissolves everything else, and puts nothing out. In a word, it is simply feelings. Everything emotional is watery by element, because it is a response to an outside stimulus, and is often not communicated. It is not, at least not in its pure sense, active or initiatory, and it does not bring anything into being unless transformed into energy of a different type, such as Fire. Cancer, Scorpio and Pisces are the Water signs, and natives of those signs are often moody, withdrawn, and uncommunicative. Their energy collects the energy of others, and keeps their mental responses to external events stored. They are not being sad for any particular reason; it is simply the way that energy works. It is quite obvious that they are not showing an outgoing energy, but neither have they anything tangible to show for their efforts, like the money and property which seem to accumulate around Earth people. Water people simply absorb, keep to themselves, and do not communicate. To the onlooker, this appears unexciting, but there again the onlooker is biased: Fire and Air energies only appreciate outgoing energy forms, Earth energies recognize material rather than mental energies, and other Water energies are staying private and self-contained!

We now recognize four kinds of energy. Each of these comes in three distinct phases; if one zodiac sign is chosen to represent each of these phases within an element, there would be twelve different kinds of energy, and that would define the zodiac of twelve, with each one showing a distinct and different phase of the same endless flow of energy.

The first phase, not surprisingly, is a phase of definition, where the energies take that form for the first time, and where they are at their purest; they are not modified by time or circumstance, and what they aim to do is to start things in their own terms. These four most powerful signs (one for each element, remember) are called cardinal signs: Aries, Cancer, Libra, Capricorn. When the Sun enters any of these signs, the seasons change; the first day of the Sun's journey through Aries is the first day of spring, and the Spring equinox; Libra marks the Autumnal equinox, while Cancer and Capricorn mark Mid-summer's Day and the shortest day respectively.

The second phase is where the energy is mature, and spreads itself a little; it is secure in its place, and the situation is well established, so there is a sort of thickening and settling of the energy flow. Here it is at its most immobile, even Air. The idea is one of maintenance and sustenance, keeping things going and keeping them strong. This stage is represented by Taurus, Leo, Scorpio, and Aquarius, and they are called, unsurprisingly, fixed signs. These four signs, and their symbols, are often taken to represent the four winds and the four directions North, South, East and West. Their symbols (with an eagle instead of a scorpion for Scorpio) turn up all over Europe as tokens for the evangelists Luke, Mark, John and Matthew (in that order).

The final phase is one of dissolution and change, as the energy finds itself applied to various purposes, and in doing so is changed into other forms. There is an emphasis on being used for the good, but being used up nonetheless. The final four signs are Gemini, Virgo, Sagittarius, and Pisces; in each of them the energies of their element are given back out for general use and benefit from where they had been maintained in the fixed phase. It is this idea of being used and changed which leads to this phase being called mutable.

Three phases of energy, then; one to form, one to grow strong and mature, and one to be used, and to become, at the end, something else. Like the waxing, full, and waning phases of the Moon.

The diagram on page 16 shows the twelve signs arranged in

their sequence round the zodiac. Notice how cleverly the cycle and phases interweave:

(a) Outgoing and collecting energies alternate, with no two the same next to each other;

(b) Physical ebb and flow are followed by mental ebb and flow alternately in pairs round the circle, meaning that the elements follow in sequence round the circle three times;

(c) Cardinal, fixed, and mutable qualities follow in sequence round the circle four times, and yet

(d) No two elements or qualities the same are next to each other, even though their sequences are not broken.

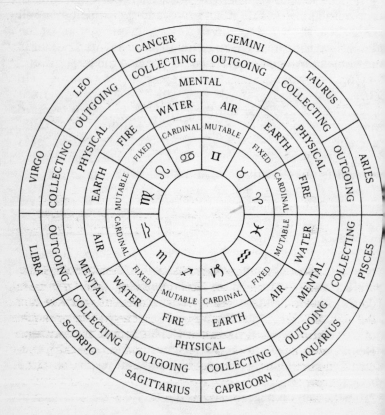

The interweaving is perfect. The zodiac shows all forms of energy, physical and mental, outgoing or incoming, waxing or waning, harmoniously forming a perfectly balanced unity when all the components are taken together. Humanity, as a whole, contains all the possibilities; each individual is a component necessary to the whole.

All this can be a bit long-winded when what you want is some way of holding all that information for instant recall and use, which is where the nine words come in.

If a single word is used for the kind of energy flow, and another two for the element and quality, then they can be used to form a sentence which will describe the way the energy is being used.

As a suggestion (use other words if they are more meaningful to you), try 'outgoing' and 'collecting' for the energy flows.

Next, for the elements:

Fire	:	activity	(Aries, Leo, Sagittarius)
Earth	:	material	(Taurus, Virgo, Capricorn)
Air	:	communication	(Gemini, Libra, Aquarius)
Water	:	feelings	(Cancer, Scorpio, Pisces)

And for the qualities:

Cardinal	:	defining	(Aries, Cancer, Libra, Capricorn)
Fixed	:	maintaining	(Taurus, Leo, Scorpio, Aquarius)
Mutable	:	using	(Gemini, Virgo, Sagittarius, Pisces)

Now in answer to the question 'What is a Gemini doing?' and answer can be formed as 'He's outgoing, and he's using communication', which neatly encapsulates the motivation of the sign. All that you need to know about the guiding principles of a Gemini individual, no matter who he is, is in that sentence. He will never deviate from that purpose, and you can adapt your own actions to partner or oppose his intention as you please.

A Scorpio? He's collecting, and he's maintaining his feelings. An Arian? He's outgoing, and he's defining activity. And so on.

Those nine words, or some similar ones which you like better, can be used to form effective and useful phrases which describe the motivation of everybody you will ever meet. How different people show it is their business, but their motivation and purpose is clear if you know their birthday.

Remember, too, that this motivation works at all levels, from the immediate to the eternal. The way a Taurean conducts himself in today's problems is a miniature of the way he is trying to achieve his medium-term ambitions over the next two or three years. It is also a miniature of his whole existence: when, as an old man, he looks back to see what he tried to do and what he achieved, both the efforts and the achievement, whatever it is, can be described in the same phrase with the same three words.

2. The Planets and the Horseshoe

You will have heard, or read, about the planets in an astrological context. You may have a horoscope in a magazine which says that Mars is here or Jupiter is there, and that as a consequence this or that is likely to happen to you. Two questions immediately spring to mind: What do the planets signify? How does that affect an individual?

The theory is straightforward again, and not as complex as that of the zodiac signs in the previous chapter. Remember that the basic theory of astrology is that since the universe and mankind are part of the same Creation, they both move in a similar fashion, so Man's movements mirror those of the heavens. So far, so good. If you look at the sky, night after night, or indeed day after day, it looks pretty much the same; the stars don't move much in relationship to each other, at least not enough to notice. What do move, though, are the Sun and Moon, and five other points of light—the planets. It must therefore follow that if these are the things which move, they must be the things which can be related to the movements of Man. Perhaps, the theory goes, they have areas of the sky in which they feel more at home, where the energy that they represent is stronger; there might be other places where they are uncomfortable and weak, corresponding to the times in your life when you just can't win no matter what you do. The planets would then behave like ludo counters, moving round the heavens trying to get back to a home of their own colour, and then starting a new game.

The scheme sounds plausible, makes a sort of common sense, and is endearingly human; all hallmarks of astrological thought, which unlike scientific thought has to relate everything to the human experience. And so it is: the planets are given values to show the universal energy in different forms, and given signs of the zodiac as homes. Therefore your Sun sign also has a planet to look after it, and the nature of that planet will show itself strongly in your character.

The planets used are the Sun and Moon, which aren't really planets at all, one being a satellite and the other a star, and then Mercury, Venus, Mars, Jupiter, and Saturn. This was enough until the eighteenth century, when Uranus was discovered, followed in the subsequent two hundred years by Neptune and Pluto. Some modern astrologers put the three new planets into horoscopes, but it really isn't necessary, and may not be such a good idea anyway. There are three good reasons for this:

(a) The modern planets break up the symmetry of the original system, which was perfectly harmonious;

(b) The old system is still good enough to describe everything that can happen in a human life, and the modern planets have little to add;

(c) Astrology is about the relationship between the sky and a human being. An ordinary human being cannot see the outer planets on his own; he needs a telescope. We should leave out of the system such things as are of an extra-human scale or magnitude: they do not apply to an ordinary human. If we put in things which are beyond ordinary human capabilities, we cannot relate them to the human experience, and we are wasting our time.

In the diagram on page 21 the zodiac is presented in its usual form, but it has also been split into two from the start of Leo to the start of Aquarius. The right hand half is called the solar half, and the other one is the lunar half. The Sun is assigned to Leo because in the Northern hemisphere, where astrology started, August is when you feel the influence of the Sun most, especially in the Eastern Mediterranean, where the Greeks and the other early Western civilizations were busy putting the framework of astrology together in the second millennium BC. The Sun is important because it gives light. The Moon gives light too; it is reflected sunlight, but it is enough to see by, and this is enough to give the Sun and Moon the title of 'the Lights' in astrology. The Moon is assigned to Cancer, so that the two of them can balance and complement each other. From there, moving away from the Lights around the circle on both sides, the signs have the planets assigned to them starting with the fastest mover, Mercury, and continuing in decreasing order of speed. Saturn is the slowest mover of all, and the two signs opposite to

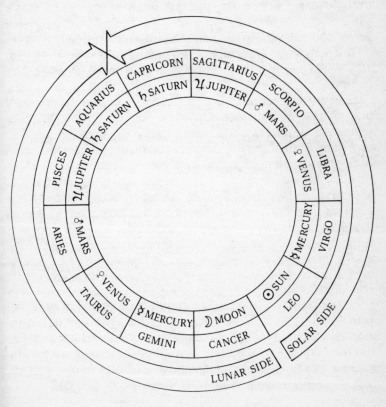

the Lights are both governed by that planet. The reasons for this apparent assymmetry will be explained in a little while. This arrangement is, of course, the horseshoe of the title to this chapter.

The Sun and Moon work in a similar fashion to the outgoing and collecting energies we noted earlier with the twelve signs. The Sun is radiant above all else; energy comes outwards from it, warming and energizing all those around it. Leo people, whose sign is the Sun's, work like this by being at the centre of a group of people and acting as inspiration and encouragement to them all. The Moon reflects the Sun's light, and energies of a lunar kind are directed inwards towards the core of the person. The two energies are necessarily linked; lunar people would starve without the solar folks' warmth, but the solar types need someone to radiate to or their purpose is unfulfilled.

The planets on each side of the horseshoe display their own energies in a solar or lunar way depending on which side of the pattern they are on.

Mercury and Venus form a pair, representing complementary but opposite ideas, which should be familiar by now. Mercury represents difference, and Venus stands for similarity.

Wherever anything new forms that is distinguishable from the background, then Mercury is there making it what it is, highlighting what makes it different. Anything separate is Mercurial, and words, since they are separate and can be strung together into millions of different combinations, are Mercurial too. Mercury is not a long-term influence; it notes things as being different for an instant, and then they become part of the establishment, and something else is new elsewhere. Because 'new' is an instantaneous state—that is, something can only be new once, and for a moment—Mercury is not associated with anything lasting, and its rapid motion as a planet leads to its being associated with the idea of speed. Virgo, Mercury's solar sign, is concerned with the changing of the shape of things ('collecting, using material' in our keyword system), while Gemini, the lunar sign, is concerned with reading and writing, and getting new ideas ('outgoing, using communication').

Venus does the reverse; it looks for that which is similar, finding points of contact to make relationships between common interests and energies. It likes to preserve the harmonies of life, and resents anything which might interrupt them. Love and affection are naturally Venusian, but so is music and all of the Arts, for the harmonies they contain. Expressed in a solar way, Venus is Libra, the maker of relationships; its lunar face is Taurus, emphasizing food and furnishings as things which give pleasure to the individual.

The next pair are Mars and Jupiter. Mars applies force from the outside to impose structure on a disordered universe, while Jupiter expands forcibly from the inside to give growth and wealth, inviting everyone else to join in.

Mars is pure force, energy in a straight line with a direction to go in. Anger and passion are both Martian, and so is lust, because they are all examples of great energy directed towards a given end. Note that Martian force is not necessarily strength, wealth, or know-how, just pure energy, which often boils over and needs controlling. Mars is the power in an athlete, and in an assassin too. It is also the power in a lover, because the urge to create is also the urge to pro-create, and if that energy fulfils its purpose then that creation takes place. Scorpio is its solar side, the power to control and create; in lunar form it is shown by Aries, as energy enjoyed for its own sake by its owner, with no purpose except to express it.

Jupiter is the spirit of expansion from within; not only does it oppose Mars' force from outside, it opposes Mars' physicality with its own mental emphasis. Jupiter develops the mind, then. As it does so, it develops all natural talents of an academic nature, and encourages movement, enquiry and travel to broaden experience and knowledge. The Solar expression of this is Sagittarius, where the centaur symbol is both a wise teacher and a free-roaming wild horse at the same time. Jupiter in a lunar sense is Pisces, where the imagination is developed to a greater extent than anywhere else, but used to provide an internal dream world for the owner's pleasure. Great sensitivity here, but the lunar energies are not of the sort to be expressed; rather other energies are *im*pressed on the Piscean mind.

Saturn is the last of the five planets. He stands alone, and if it is necessary to consider him as paired with anything it is with the Lights as an entity together. The Lights are at the centre of the system; Saturn is at its edge. They are the originators of the energies of the zodiac, and he is the terminator. Everything to do with limits and ends is his. He represents Time, and lots of it, in contrast to Mercury, which represented the instant. He represents the sum total of all things, and the great structures and frameworks of long-term endeavour. In solar form he is Capricorn, the representative of hard work, all hierarchies, and all rulers; in lunar form he is Aquarius, showing the horizontal structure of groups of people within society at different levels. Here he denies the activity of Mars, because society is too big for one person to change against the collective will, and he contains the expansion of Jupiter within himself. Venus and Mercury can neither relate to it nor make it change, because it is always the same, in the end.

The planets show important principles in action, the same as the zodiac does. You have probably noticed that the horseshoe of the planets and the ring of the zodiac say the same thing in a different way, and that is true about most things in astrology. It may be that the two systems interrelate and overlap because they are from the same source: after all, $3+2+2=7$, which is the planet's total, and $3x2x2=12$, which is the signs'. How you assign the elements and qualities, pairs of planets and lights is for you to decide. The joy of astrology, like all magic, is that it has you at the centre, and is made to fit its user's requirements. Now you know the principles, you can use it as you please, and as it seems relevant to you.

Part 2

Yourself—and Others

3. The Essential Scorpio

All the energy in the zodiac is solar, but that solar energy takes many forms. It is moderated and distributed through the planetary energies until it finally shows in you, the individual. As a Scorpio, the prime planetary energy is that of Mars; you will be motivated by, and behave in the manner of, the energies of Mars. To remind yourself of what that means, read the section on Mars on page 22. As a sign of the zodiac, Scorpio is a fixed Water sign. Remind yourself what that means by reading page 17. Now we have to see how those essential principles work when expressed through a person and his motivation.

What it Means to be a Scorpio

You know what it is to be a Scorpio, because you are one; but you probably don't know what it is that makes a Scorpio the way he is, because you cannot stand outside yourself. You would have to be each of the other eleven signs in turn to understand the nature of the energy that motivates you. This essential energy is in every Scorpio, but it shows itself to different extents and in different ways. Because it is in every single Scorpio, it is universal rather than specific, and universal ideas tend to come in language which sounds a little on the woolly side. You will think that it isn't really about what makes you who you are, because you don't feel like that every day—or at least you think you don't. In fact, you feel like that all the time, but you don't notice it any more than you notice your eyes focusing, yet they do it all the time, and you see things the way you do because of it.

The first thing to note is that the zodiac is a circle, not a line with a beginning and an end. If it were a line, then Scorpio would be about two-thirds of the way along it, but that would be to miss the point; if the zodiac is a circle, then Scorpio is a stage in an endlessly repeating cycle, and we will get a much better idea of what it is if we look to see where it came from, and where it is going.

The sign before Scorpio is Libra. Libra represents the individual's concern to form relationships with others, and it does this by offering itself in friendship. Libra is the initiator of all relationships, and is more than willing to change its point of view, or make the odd adjustment here and there, if the end result is helpful to the relationship. To a certain extent, this makes Librans pliable, but only because they have to be to achieve their ends. At all times they are concerned that the energies of the situation be balanced. Not necessarily static, but balanced, which is how they would like to see it.

Scorpio is a development from that stance. Where Libra started the relationship, and sent out the invitations, so to speak, then Scorpio has to handle the returns, evaluate the responses, decide on his responses in turn, and do what he can to keep the situation under control and growing nicely. Where Libra gives out an idea, Scorpio collects the reply, or the feeling it generates. Scorpio collects all that there is about a situation, and makes sure that it is all going the way he wants it to. Nothing is left to chance: interpersonal relationships are a minefield, in the Scorpio view, best handled by a professional such as himself.

There will come a time, possibly, when Scorpio is so much in control of things that he will cease to consider the possibility of anything going wrong. He will know that he can cope with anything, and he will be well enough informed about virtually everything to be able to give help and advice to others, without having to worry about himself. When he reaches that stage of confidence, he will have left Scorpio and become a Sagittarian, the next phase in the cycle. For now, however, we must concentrate on the Scorpio's existence as he devotes himself to controlling the situation Libra left him in.

If we go back to the basic structures of astrology, we see that Scorpio is a collecting sign rather than an outgoing one. This means, Scorpio, that you are taking things in from your situation, rather than contributing to it. You react to the things around you, and especially to the people you contact. Scorpio is also a Water sign; this means that the world you choose to operate in is not a material one, but a mental one. Impressions, emotions, feelings; motivations, desires, needs; jealousies, revenges. These are the features of the Scorpionic landscape, the features of your daily existence that are prominent landmarks, and which you recognize and navigate by. This emphasis on the mental world makes you intelligent, and naturally so: Nature sees to it that animals get the equipment they need to suit them for their environment. Taureans are Earth creatures and have the strength and stamina necessary to exist in a material world; you have the intelligence and cunning necessary to exist in a world of feelings and emotional responses.

Scorpio is also a Fixed sign: you like your environment, and you find that you can manipulate it or work with it so that you can gain profit from it. You feel safe and familiar among the hopes and fears of others; you know that with a little bit of effort here, and a bit of care there, you can make them grow the way you want. Like the gardener who makes his vegetables grow bigger with care and attention, so you work with the motivation of your companions. What you want out of it is the security of being in control: the idea of not being in control terrifies you.

What you are trying to do is to maintain your emotional responses to things at the level they are now at. You think, somehow, that if you get over-emotional about things you will lose precious emotional energy, which must be kept intact. You are right, to some extent; you have a very great deal of emotional energy, but you are not a generator of it, as the Cancerian is, nor does it benefit you to let it loose and be swept away on it, in the

Piscean manner. To do so would be contrary to the nature of your ruling planet, Mars; Mars gives things firm direction. Letting things loose is not Martian.

So, to maintain your emotional response, you make sure that you are familiar with what's going on. That way nothing will surprise you, shock you, sneak up on you, or in any other way cause an uncontrolled emotional reaction. To do this you need to anticipate everybody's moves. You have to find out about everybody else and be able to see what they're going to do *before* they do it. You also have to maintain control of the environment, so that nothing unexpected can occur from outside so change people's anticipated response. This is going to mean a lot of work, but you know that it is the only way, and so you do it. Total control, of yourself, your surroundings, and everybody else. When you've got that, you're happy. You will have picked up, en route, so to speak, the skills of a detective, a psychiatrist, and the secret police, as well as the organizational and financial skills of a business analyst and investment consultant; but these are actually secondary: the prime aim is to maintain control of your own emotional responses.

It needs a lot of energy and determination to do all the things you have set for yourself, and to do them at the deep levels necessary for your purposes; luckily, Mars gives you that. Mars is the energy you use to investigate things, find out how they work, and (most importantly) how they are likely to affect you. Mars is also the destructive power you unleash on your enemies, hurting them before they can hurt you. Your are better than they are at plotting and scheming, because you are at home in the world of the imagination, where they are probably not, and their passions and jealousies are easily recognized by you as more emotional energy for you to collect and use. You don't leave them anything like so easy a way into your own way of thinking: you have it under control, of course.

The Scorpio is a creature whose impact in the imagination is much bigger than his physical presence and capabilities. He induces fear and fascination in the onlooker, and seems to enjoy it; when disturbed he is lethal. He is difficult to see the inside of, because he armours himself against intruders. Only when the situation is completely beyond his control will his reserve break, and then his anger is as likely to be directed against himself, for letting the situation get like that, as against his enemies. All of these things apply to the animal after which the sign is named just as much as to any Scorpio individual—there is no better picture of a Scorpio than a scorpion.

Early, Middle or Late? The Decanates

Each of the zodiac signs is divided into degrees like an arc of any other circle. Since a circle has 360 degrees, then each sign must be 30 degrees, since there are twelve signs. Each of the signs is further split into sections of ten degrees, called decanates. There are three decanates in each sign, and the one that your birthday falls in will tell you a little more about how that Scorpionic energy actually works in you as an individual.

First decanate (23 October–1 November)
This is the purest form of Scorpio. There is a double helping of Martian energy here, giving a particularly intense desire to exercise a controlling influence. Scorpio is the sign associated with beginnings and endings; where the essence of things come from, and where they go, is a spiritual question rather than a physical one, and in astrology the Water signs deal with spiritual energies for the most part. Scorpio is the deepest Water sign, and so all the unknown answers to the great mysteries are in it somewhere. This section of the sign, then, is concerned with the processes of life and death. Perhaps you will be literally concerned with them; undertakers and obstetricians both have a Scorpionic role in life. Perhaps your own life will be played out in separate sections, with each episode having to be completed before the next can begin. Such people have no lifelong friends, and no real roots, because they must surrender them all at the end of each stage of their life. Scorpios are particularly good at making new beginnings, and this end of the sign emphasizes that characteristic. It is all because of the Martian energy: Mars

defines and delimits, being both energizer and executioner.

Second decanate (2–11 November)

Here the energy and capacity to give and take life, symbolized by Mars, is blended with the energy of Jupiter, which causes it to spread and dissipate. None of the energy is lost, and the energy is not lessened by its being spread over a greater area: if you want a mental picture, imagine a drop of ink falling into a glass of water, spreading out to mingle with the clear liquid, turning it to its own colour. The fact that it all happens below the surface is of interest, as is the fact that the ink permeates the water completely, leaving none of it untouched. The Scorpio from this decanate is interested in the underlying causes of things and likes to penetrate beneath the surface of what he sees, to discover their true identity. He spreads out, too, until he has discovered and examined every part of the origins of things. The early decanate Scorpio is publicly visible, but this one keeps a very low profile indeed.

There are one or two things assigned to this section of the sign which may remind you of the ink in the water, and may prove to be suitable symbols for events in your life: among them are all mutations, irreversible changes, and transformations, and all forms of poison or venom.

Third decanate (12–21 November)

The last decanate of Scorpio finds the energies of Mars mixed with those of the Moon. This is a very unusual combination, for these two planets are usually particularly averse to each other's company. The powerfully individual energy of Mars becomes reflected outwards by that of the Moon, and is put to use for the benefit of others. Often this takes the form of things handed on from one generation to another; you may be involved in handing something on, or you may be the recipient of such a legacy. The extension of a family, as it descends from one generation into another, is to do with this end of the sign; your position in the dynasty, so to speak, may be important to you if your birthday is here.

Scorpio knows that making the best use of all the resources at his command is his special talent, and he knows, too, that things go in stages, often with no possibility of keeping things from one stage to another. So he is quite willing, in this decanate, to put his talents to use for the benefit of those whom he may never meet. Bankers, and others who handle other people's money, are assigned to this part of the sign, not surprisingly; it is all to do with controlling resources *on behalf of other people* – an interesting change of emphasis as the zodiac prepares to leave Scorpio for Sagittarius.

Three Phases of Life: Scorpio as Child, Adult, Parent

The Scorpio child
Perseverance and determination are not usually the qualities expected of a child, but a young Scorpio has plenty of both. When he finds something to take his interest, he will spend a great deal of time with it; this is not the sort of child whose interest span is only a few minutes, and who is always looking for something new. Even if there are difficulties in mastering the activity in question, he will stay with it until he has control of it.

Scorpio children are deeply curious. They need to know all that there is to know about the things which interest them. All children are curious, of course, but where the Virgo child likes to know how things work, and the Sagittarian child just likes to know lots of things (the scope matters more than the depth to him), the Scorpio child wants to know the underlying reasons why. It's not the knowing that he particularly enjoys; it's the finding out. Scorpio children, therefore, love mystery stories, and, when they are a little older, detective fiction.

Once he has established a way of doing things to his satisfaction, the young Scorpio is very unwilling to change. He will be quite sure in his own mind, no matter how young he is, that he has covered all the eventualities, and is going about things in the most effective and productive way. Having to abandon his routines, therefore, results in a display of stubbornness. Often labelled sulky, moody or spiteful for their behaviour,

Scorpio children are none of these; what is being described is determined and purposive behaviour on a child's scale, seen from an adult's viewpoint.

The young Scorpio practises self-control, which is such a feature of his adult life, from a very early age. Consequently, he recognizes, and appreciates, any behaviour-controlling environment. In other words, he actually flourishes under a strict upbringing, unlike virtually every other zodiacal youngster of the twelve.

The Scorpio adult

Scorpio adults are getting to be more and more effective as this century goes on. Let me explain. Now that most European societies are highly developed, and most of us live in cities, there isn't a lot of space. The most successful individuals are going to be the ones who don't have to wave their arms about to be effective, and who don't find the prospect of a lifetime working in the middle ranks of a large company too depressing for words. These well-adapted individuals are going to have to be very good at handling people, very good at getting their own way despite the opposition and apathy of the world at large, and practically invisible: Scorpios are all of these.

No zodiac sign has more stamina than Scorpio. Mars gives power to Aries too, but the Arian's actions are based on explosive release of energy, while the Scorpio's are based on concentrated application. It's the difference between dynamite and a cutting torch; they both open safes, but one is more controlled, although the other's faster.

Scorpios do not waste time. Time, like money, is a resource, and is therefore to be used effectively and sparingly, in your way of thinking. You decide what you want, think round it until you are fully conversant with every possible aspect of it, including what might happen if things go wrong, and then use the means at your disposal in the most effective and concentrated way to achieve your purpose. What you don't know is that other signs just don't have that degree of intensity, that capacity for concentration, or that kind of sheer power.

You build your life in a series of little steps, each one with a goal to be achieved or a target to be met. When you have succeeded (only a matter of time), you can go to the next. You fit very well into large organizations; their restrictive structure is a familiar framework of control to you, and you direct your energies through that framework so that your way of working is its way of working. This means that you probably rise quickly through the organization; if you do not, it is because you are satisfied with whatever you have found at the level you have reached, and are unwilling to change.

Whatever you do, and wherever you do it, you are always in control; you will venture nothing which might involve you not being in control, not even for a minute. That's the key to the adult Scorpio: the controlled application of concentrated energy. Everything else follows on from that.

The Scorpio parent

Scorpio parents have only one fault—inflexibility. They are very proud of their children: they have a fondness for them, which comes from being a Water sign, and they are thrilled to think that the family is continuing and growing, which comes from being a Fixed sign. They provide a carefully controlled environment for their children to grow up in, but the children themselves, unless Scorpios like their parents, may find this too restrictive.

Children usually like to do things their own way, and it is here that the inflexibility of the Scorpio parent shows. He is unable to see that his carefully considered and proven ways of doing things hold no appeal for his children, and of course, the more he tries to force his point of view, the worse things get. The sense of injury to the parent is twofold: firstly, he is upset to think that his own efforts are not fully appreciated by the very audience whose approval he most desires, and secondly he is aghast to to think of the waste of time his children are about to embark upon to come to (he thinks) the same conclusions he came to years ago. The simple realization that his own way is only best for him would help matters a great deal.

4. Scorpio Relationships

How Zodiacal Relationships Work

You might think that relationships between two people, described in terms of their zodiac signs, might come in 144 varieties; that is, twelve possible partners for each of the twelve signs. The whole business is a lot simpler than that. There are only seven varieties of relationship, although each of those has two people in it, of course, and the role you play depends on which end of the relationship you are at.

You may well have read before about how you are supposed to be suited to one particular sign or another. The truth is usually different. Scorpios are supposed to get on with Pisceans and Cancerians, and indeed they do, for the most part, but it is no use reading that if you have always found yourself attracted to Geminis, is it? There has to be a reason why you keep finding Geminis attractive, and it is not always to do with your Sun sign; other factors in your horoscope will have a lot to do with it. The reason you prefer people of certain signs as friends or partners is because the relationship of your sign to theirs produces the sort of qualities you are looking for, the sort of behaviour you find satisfactory. When you have identified which of the seven types of basic relationship it is, you can see which signs will produce that along with your own, and then read the motivation behind it explained later on in more detail in 'The Scorpio Approach to Relationships' and the individual compatibility sections.

Look at the diagram on page 16. All you have to do is see how far away from you round the zodiacal circle your partner's Sun sign is. If they are Aries, they are five signs in front of you. You are also, of course, five signs behind them, which is also important, as you will see in a little while. If they are Leo, they are three signs behind you, and you are three signs in front of them. There are seven possibilities: you can be anything up to six signs apart, or you can both be of the same sign.

Here are the patterns of behaviour for the seven relationship types.

Same sign

Somebody who is of the same sign as you acts in the same way that you do, and is trying to achieve the same result for himself. If your goals permit two winners, this is fine, but if only one of you can be on top, you will argue. No matter how temperamental, stubborn, devious, or critical you can be, they can be just the same, and it may not be possible for you to take the same kind of punishment you hand out to others. In addition, they will display every quality which really annoys you about yourself, so that you are constantly reminded of it in yourself as well as in them. Essentially, you are fighting for the same space, and the amount of tolerance you have is the determining factor in the survival of this relationship.

One sign apart

Someone one sign forward from you acts as an environment for you to grow in. In time, you will take on those qualities yourself. When you have new ideas, they can often provide the encouragement to put them into practice, and seem to have all your requirements easily available. Often, it is this feeling that they already know all the pitfalls that you are struggling over which can be annoying; they always seem to be one step ahead of you, and can seemingly do without effort all the things which you have to sweat to achieve. If the relationship works well, they are helpful to you, but there can be bitterness and jealousy if it doesn't.

Someone one sign back from you can act as a retreat from the pressures of the world. They seem to understand your particular needs for rest and recovery, whatever they may be, and can usually provide them. They can hold and understand your innermost secrets and fears; indeed, their mind works best with the things you fear most, and the fact that they can handle these so easily is a great help to you. If the relationship is going through a bad patch, their role as controller of your fears gets worrying, and you will feel unnerved in their presence, as though they were in control of you. When things are good, you feel secure with them behind you.

Two signs apart
Someone two signs forward from you acts like a brother or sister. They are great friends, and you feel equals in each other's company; there is no hint of the parent-child or master-servant relationship. They encourage you to talk, even if you are reticent in most other company; the most frequently heard description of these relationships is 'We make each other laugh'. Such a partner can always help you put into words the things that you want to say, and is there to help you say them. This is the relationship that teenagers enjoy with their 'best friend'. There is love, but it does not usually take sexual form, because both partners know that it would spoil the relationship by adding an element of unnecessary depth and weight.

Someone two signs behind you is a good friend and companion, but not as intimate as somebody two signs forward. They are the sort of people you love to meet socially; they are reliable and honest, but not so close that things become suffocatingly intense. They stop you getting too serious about life, and turn your thoughts outwards instead of inwards, involving you with other people. They stop you from being too selfish, and help you give the best of yourself to others. This relationship, then, has a cool end and a warm end; the leading sign feels much closer to his partner than the trailing sign does, but they are both satisfied by the relationship. They particularly value its chatty quality, the fact that it works even better when in a group, and its tone of affection and endearment rather than passion and obsession.

Three signs apart
Someone three signs in front of you represents a challenge of some kind or another. The energies of the pair of you can never run parallel, and so must meet at some time or another. Not head on, but across each other, and out of this you can both make something strong and well established which will serve the two of you as a firm base for the future. You will be surprised to find how fiercely this person will fight on your behalf, or for your protection; you may not think you need it, and you will be surprised that anybody would think of doing it, but it is so nonetheless.

Someone three signs behind you is also a challenge, and for the same reasons as stated above; from this end of the relationship, though, they will help you achieve the very best you are capable of in a material sense. They will see to it that you receive all the credit that is due to you for your efforts, and that everyone thinks well of you. Your reputation is their business, and they will do things with it that you could never manage yourself. It's like having your own P.R. team. This relationship works hard, gets results, and makes sure the world knows it. It also looks after itself, but it needs a lot of effort putting in.

Four signs apart
Someone four signs forward from you is the expression of yourself. All the things you wanted to be, however daring, witty, sexy, or whatever, they already are, and you can watch them doing it. They can also help you to be these things. They do things which you think are risky, and seem to get away with them. There are things you aim towards, sometimes a way of life that you would like to have, which these people seem to be able to live all the time; it doesn't seem to worry them that things might go wrong. There are lots of things in their life which frighten you, which you would lie awake at nights worrying about, which they accept with a child's trust, and which never go

wrong for them. You wish you could be like that.

Someone four signs behind you is an inspiration to you. All the things you wish you knew, they know already. They seem so wise and experienced, and you feel such an amateur; luckily, they are kind and caring teachers. They are convincing, too. When they speak, you listen and believe. It's nice to know there's somebody there with all the answers. This extraordinary relationship often functions as a mutual admiration society, with each end wishing it could be more like the other; unfortunately, it is far less productive than the three-sign separation, and much of its promise remains unfulfilled. Laziness is one of the inherent qualities of a four-sign separation; all its energies are fulfilled, and it rarely looks outside itself for something to act upon. Perhaps this is just as well for the rest of us.

Five signs apart
Someone five signs ahead of you is your technique. You know what you want to do; this person knows how to do it. He can find ways and means for you to do what you want to be involved in, and he can watch you while you learn and correct your mistakes. They know the right way to go about things, and have the clarity of thought and analytical approach necessary if you are to get things clear in your mind before you get started

Someone five signs behind you is your resource. Whenever you run out of impetus or energy, they step forward and support you. When you're broke, they lend you money, and seldom want it returned. When you need a steadying hand because you think you've over-reached yourself, they provide it. All this they do because they know that it's in their best interest as well as yours, to help you do things, and to provide the material for you to work with. You can always rely on them for help, and it's nice to know they will always be there. They cannot use all their talent on their own; they need you to show them how it should be done. Between you, you will use all that you both have to offer effectively and fully, but it is a relationship of cooperation and giving; not all the zodiac signs can make it work well enough.

Six signs apart

Someone six signs apart from you, either forwards or backwards, is both opponent and partner at the same time. You are both essentially concerned with the same area of life, and have the same priorities. Yet you both approach your common interests from opposite directions, and hope to use them in opposite ways. Where one is private, the other is public, and where one is self-centred, the other shares himself cheerfully. The failings in your own make-up are complemented by the strengths in the other; it is as if, between you, you make one whole person with a complete set of talents and capabilities. The problem with this partnership is that your complementary talents focus the pair of you on a single area of life, and this makes for not only a narrow outlook, but also a lack of flexibility in your response to changes. If the two of you are seeing everything in terms of career, or property, or personal freedom, or whatever, then you will have no way to deal effectively with a situation which cannot be dealt with in those terms. Life becomes like a seesaw; it alternates which end it has up or down, and can sometimes stay in balance; but it cannot swing round to face another way, and it is fixed to the ground so that it does not move.

These are the only combinations available, and all partnerships between two people can be described as a version of one of the seven types. It must be remembered, though, that some of the roles engendered by these dispositions of sign to sign are almost impossible to fulfil for some of the signs, because their essential energies, and the directions they are forced to take by the planets behind them, drive them in ways which make it too difficult. To form a relationship based on sharing and acceptance is one thing: to do it when you are governed by a planet like Mars is somethings else. Even when the relationship can form, the sort of approach produced by, say, Jupiter, is a very different thing from that produced by Venus.

The next thing you must consider, then, is how you, as an Arian, attempt relationships as a whole, and what you try to find in them. Then you must lay the qualities and outlook of each of the twelve signs over the roles they must play in the seven relationship types, and see whether the pair of you manage to make the best of that relationship, or not.

The seven relationship types are common to all the signs, relating to all the other signs. You can use your understanding of them to analyse and understand the relationship between any pair of people that you know, whether or not they are a Scorpio; but to see how the characters fit into the framework in more detail, you will need to look at the individual compatibilities, of which just the Arian ones are given in this book.

The next thing you must consider, then, is how you, as a Scorpio, attempt relationships as a whole, and what you try to find in them. Then you must lay the qualities and outlook of each of the twelve signs over the roles they must play in the seven relationship types, and see whether the pair of you manage to make the best of that relationship, or not.

The seven relationship types are common to all the signs, relating to all the other signs. You can use your understanding of them to analyse and understand the relationship between any pair of people that you know, whether or not they are a Scorpio; but to see how the characters fit into the framework in more detail, you will need to look at the individual compatibilities, of which just the Scorpio ones are given in this book.

The Scorpio Approach to Relationships

All Scorpios are sexy. Everybody knows this; in fact it's about all that anybody ever says about a Scorpio. Is it true? If so, why is it true? Does it say something about the way Scorpios approach their relationships?

The answers to those questions are yes, because of Mars; but that isn't the whole story.

The way to fathom a Scorpio's approach to relationships is firstly to determine what it is that he wants to get out of them, and then to see how he goes about making sure he does so. To start with, as in everything else in his life, the Scorpio wants to control the situation, and within that, his partner. He does this by applying his energies in a concentrated and effective way. Viewed from the other end, from the partner's point of view, this seems magnetically attractive. It is: any energy directed your way is welcome, and you tend to turn towards anyone giving out energy for free. Since Scorpio energy is an essentially emotional energy (that of the element of Water), directed and aimed in a personal and physical manner (because Mars powers the physical body), it is interpreted by the other eleven signs as the only powerful physical/emotional energy they know—sexual energy. Understand this: other signs only meet this kind of energy, or use it, in a sexual context, but Scorpios use it all the time, and not always for sex; it just happens to be the only energy they have available.

So yes, Scorpios are sexy; they radiate the energy that everybody recognizes as sexual energy. This means that everybody responds in a sexual manner to a Scorpio, which is to say in an emotionally heightened state. Scorpio loves this; it means that the whole transaction is conducted on an emotional level, which is the level on which he functions best of all. This means, of course, that he gets his own way, because he is much more familiar with manipulating emotions than anybody else, and indeed can use them as a kind of fuel. By using that kind of energy to start with, he forces his partner in the relationship to respond in the same kind, whether or not they would naturally do so. It's a similar process to the card game where the player who leads can declare the trump suit, and proceeds to win every trick in the game because every card in his hand is of that suit. This is how Scorpios get to be so successful, and so dominant. It is a self-repeating process which favours the Scorpio every time: clever, isn't it?

When it does come to sex, the Scorpio is still ahead; sexual relationships are about reproduction, basically, and that means the element of Water and the power of Mars, representing the masculine principle. Scorpio combines the two. Mars is the masculine action in sex; the feminine actions are shared between Venus and the Moon. Mars is dominant, assertive, and penetrating, and this means that Scorpio men find sexual expression quite easy. A Scorpio woman often gets a reputation as something of a man-eater, and it isn't difficult to see why; Mars' way of expressing its energies means that she has to be assertive and dominant. She can't be penetrating physically, and so has to express that trait of Mars by her behaviour in controlling the relationship. This is absolutely true to Scorpio: her reputation, if she has one, is entirely due to society's poor understanding of the way Scorpio works.

There is a part of the body assigned to each zodiac sign, too, and in Scorpio's case it is the genital organs. It is possible, as you will no doubt have realized, to have too much of a good thing. The symbolism goes further than the obvious, though: if you think how genital organs work you will have a very good idea of why a Scorpio behaves the way he does. They are usually hidden from view, for a start, and Scorpios are rather secretive people. The urges they produce are all emotional, but they are the strongest we know; people change their whole lives in response to these urges. What these organs produce is a limited resource (women have a finite number of egg cells), but it is highly concentrated, and using only a little of it has enormous results. It is also to do with the very substance of life; generation and regeneration can only occur through these organs. Scorpio is like that. Everything to him has that same sense of significance. Genital organs are serious things, concerned with life-and-death matters; using them involves the deepest parts of our being, and astrology being what it is, the deepest parts of mankind and the universe, too. Scorpios represent those energies to the rest of society in personal form—hence the intensity, the seriousness, and the sheer, concentrated power.

So now you see that Scorpios have to use sexual energy for more purposes than sex, and that the intensity of this energy and the way it is used means that they become dominant over a partner who is not as familiar with this kind of energy as they are. The question still remains, though: what is the Scorpio trying to achieve?

The answer is the same as it was on page 17: he wants to maintain and control his emotional responses. He needs to be appreciated; he wants the reassurance of a continuing flow of emotional responses from other people to comfort and sustain him. He collects, and indeed exists on, this emotional approval; unlike the Cancerian, who generates his own emotional energies in response to the actions of others, or the Piscean, who uses the emotions of others as a vehicle for his own amusement, the Scorpio needs to define and sustain himself by collecting the responses of others, and of course, he needs them to be both favourable and constant. What he is trying to do to achieve this is, firstly, to concentrate and use his energy so that his efforts always result in a response favourable to him, and secondly, somehow to keep and store his own emotional energy because it is so precious to him.

Scorpios have to keep most of their energy locked in. It is a bit like hydro-electric power: there is a great amount of water kept behind a dam, released in a controlled manner to be used profitably. If all the water is released, then disaster occurs; similarly, if all the water is used up, there is none left to meet future needs.

A Scorpio examines every relationship as it forms. 'How much will I have to give to this?' he asks himself. 'Will it mean that I have to give more than I get in return?' If so, it's a bad idea, because the net emotional balance shows a loss, and I must keep things in reserve, or augment them if possible. Will I get so carried away that I may use my energy in an uncontrolled manner, and so leave myself vulnerable when I least expect it? If so, I had better keep my involvement, or at least my commitment, under close watch, to prevent such a situation developing.' The need to conserve and control never leaves him. His greatest fear is being out of control. Quite straightforward, really: if a Scorpio is dedicated to the idea of control, then being out of that state is what he would most like to avoid.

The best way for the Scorpio to keep himself under control is to retreat a little, to bury himself under the surface out of the way of unfriendly eyes. What this means, of course, is that he never gives himself entirely to his partner, but always keeps a little in reserve. It is this hidden reserve, where his most secret self lives, that is never risked by exposing it to something as unstable as somebody else's care.

The reserved self doesn't need the stimulation or support of another person's energy, or at any rate it isn't allowed to. Consequently, Scorpios have difficulty forming deep and lasting relationships. It isn't because they aren't used to dealing with emotions, as most people seem to think; it's because they are not prepared to commit themselves entirely to another person. For this reason Scorpios form strong and successful business partnerships, but fewer good personal partnerships.

Friendships with a Scorpio form not from a desire for companionship, but because the two people are useful to each other or have a shared interest. The energy flow is inwards rather than outwards, you see. Sexual friendships are similar: the Scorpio has more than enough sexual power for anybody, but the emotional response he offers alongside the physical partnership will be very strictly controlled, and not every partner will be prepared to accept that. As for marriage, it hasn't much appeal when one partner can look after himself quite well and is unwilling to give himself fully to his partner.

The last few paragraphs paint a bleak picture. It isn't as bad as it sounds, but it does show that the popular version of the Scorpio's capabilities seldom considers the problem from both sides, as the Scorpio himself would. In those areas of a relationship where intensity of energy is a bonus, the Scorpio is unbeatable; but he suffers, or certainly seems to, as far as the rest of us are concerned, by being unable to enjoy those areas of a relationship which are light and free from care.

Individual Compatibilities Sign by Sign

All relationships between the signs work in the way described earlier in 'How Zodiacal Relationships Work'. In addition to that, descriptions of how a Scorpio attempts to form a relationship with someone from each of the twelve signs are given below. I have tried to show not what a Capricorn, for example, is like, but what a Scorpio sees him as, and how he sees you. Each individual Capricorn looks different, of course, but their motivation is the same, and these descriptions are meant to help you understand what you are trying to do with them, and how they are trying to handle you. As usual, the words he and his can be taken to mean she and her, since astrology makes no distinctions in sex here.

Scorpio-Aries

This is a relationship which should give you plenty to think about. You live in different universes, you have different targets, and the things you both consider vitally important don't even exist in the other one's way of thinking; you have absolutely nothing in common at all—except for the fact that you are both driven by the same planet, Mars. You will be fascinated to compare yourself with the Arian, and amazed to see how the same familiar energy works in such an unfamiliar fashion through him.

Aries lives for the moment. He never plans forwards, and he very seldom looks back to see what he has done in the past. Each moment is full of opportunity in his view, and there is an infinity of new possibilities open to him. What matters to him is not what could happen if he did *not* do something, but what he could achieve if he *did* do something. His view of things is intensely personal: it never occurs to him that other people's reactions or intentions are in any way relevant to his own existence. He exists for himself first, and makes the assumption (wrongly) that everybody else must be doing the same.

You will recognize his energy and his drive, but it will seem strange to you that he appears to use it in an unconsidered fashion. It is not really so: he lives in a world where emotions are not so important as they are to you. He only really exists when he is in action; the action itself gives him purpose and direction, and so he tries to be active all the time, because that way he stays in contact with himself, and knows who he is. It is your emotions and your mind that are the most important thing to you, but it is his body which is the most important thing to him. Where you would like to think around a problem, using your mind, and testing your emotional responses to it in various ways, he would like to use his body to attack the problem directly, by physically doing something about it.

Physical energy is powerful and immediate, but it is not subtle. You will probably find the Arian too trusting, and even rather naïve. Be careful in your analysis: Arians are not great thinkers, but they are not unintelligent, even though their mind is not their greatest asset. Carefully laid arrangements of intrigue and secrecy can be shredded by one bold stroke from the simple and honest Arian. His greatest weapon against you, but one of which he is entirely unaware, is his spontaneity; he can do anything he wants at a moment's notice, and probably will. You cannot possibly allow for that in your careful assessments, and it would be useless to try.

In many ways you admire him; he has a capacity for getting things done and converting thought into action which you don't have. It is simply a matter of your elements and qualities: Aries is Fire, and so can make the material world we live in move the way he wants it. He is also cardinal, and so can impose his will upon things to provide new beginnings at any time. You have the ability to start again, too, which you get from Mars as Aries does, but you cannot make a new situation from nothing: you are not an originator, which he is.

You see him as willpower in action, the personification of your own concentrated energy. He sees you as the master of all the things he intends to look into some day when he gets a minute, because he knows that they are somehow important.

If you want him as a friend, you will have to be more outgoing; he isn't prepared to play intricate and intimate games. If it's not easy to see at once, he isn't interested, and so you will have to arrange things so that he sees enough to catch his eye. You will be infuriated at his transparent simplicity of outlook, and he will be puzzled by how closely you examine everything. The only thing you will actually feel at home with in each other is the intensity of energy, supplied by Mars. Mars will also help you form a strong and energetic sexual relationship, one which you will enjoy very much. Aries uses his body rather than his mind in sex, and he won't notice you keeping your true, emotional, self out of the relationship. That's fine as far as you are concerned, and you need have no fear about overwhelming him with your forceful Martian energy—he's every bit as strong.

Marriage? Not really—at the end of the day he doesn't really understand you, and if he did, he wouldn't like it. Similarly, you can't live with his childish trust and simplicity on a long-term basis, either. As a business partnership, though, it's brilliant.

Scorpio-Taurus

Pairings of opposite signs run into difficulties more because of the similarities of the signs than because of the differences. At the same time, those similarities give the relationship a much greater chance of success than you might think. This one is no exception; you are both cautious souls, moving in a deliberate manner after due consideration, and you both feel a lot safer when you are surrounded by things which you can call your own. Novelty and instability bother you both.

Taurus is much more concerned with material things than you are, but that doesn't mean that he is insensitive to the world of the emotions. Far from it. Taurus is very sensitive indeed to what people think of him or say to him, but it is not his way to show it. You will understand this very well because you, too, keep your emotions well hidden. He will be wounded quite deeply when criticized, but because he endures the pain in silence he gets a reputation for being thick-skinned. You will know, as a representative of an animal whose insides are so sensitive that you need a shell to keep them safe, how he must feel. The great difference between you comes in what you do in response to that injury. You, Scorpio, bury yourself in a secret world of plot and counter-plot, thinking all the time about how to ensure firstly that you are never hurt again, and secondly that you are always in a position of control over your enemies. Taurus simply retreats, and comforts himself with physical pleasures. A lot of Taureans use food as a comforter, or the pleasure of having a beautiful house where they feel secure, or the enjoyment of beautiful possessions that are unchanged by unkind words. Taurus puts his trust in material things in a way that you don't.

You will find him thoughtful and reliable, but you will also find him slow. Taureans are much more willing to accept things as they are than you, and they will simply sit out difficult circumstances, waiting for better times to come along, where you would be working hard to advance yourself from that position to a better one.

They find you careful and thoughtful, which they like, but deep and unfathomable, which they don't. Rather than try to plumb the depths of your fixed Water (they would drown in the attempt), they decide that as long as you are no threat to their physical well-being they will be happy to stay with you and enjoy what bits of you they can.

A friendship between you will probably form as a sort of mutual defence arrangement—what you will like most about each other to begin with will be that you don't have to be continually on the defensive. After that, you will develop the friendship through the growing sense of reliability and support that you each find in the other.

There is a very strong sexual attraction between you, but it is a bit on the slow side, because it comes from so deep down inside you. There will be no brilliant flashes of sexual electricity; at your level the energy is more like that of a volcano, in that massive heat builds up over a long time. The union is likely to be fertile and fruitful; it's what you get if you Water your Earth!

As a marriage, this one would work well, because your energies will continue to grow towards each other over a very long period of time; some relationships are definitely short-term, but this one isn't. Once Scorpio has learned that he can trust Taurus, he need not be suspicious and can turn his energies towards making a successful life for the two of them. Taurus will provide stability, support, and warm affection for the team.

As a business partnership, this one is less good: it lacks the inventiveness and confidence necessary to make profitable progress.

Scorpio-Gemini

On the surface there isn't a lot of contact between these two signs. Gemini is an Air sign; to you he seems to be insubstantial and not to take things seriously enough. He seems to have no emotions that you can gather in and work with. He is also mutable, and therefore readily accepts change for its own sake. In fact, you can't get hold of him at all, and that exasperates you.

You don't have to get hold of him, though. He will come to you of his own accord, because he is interested in the way you work. Like the birds that follow the ploughman, he wants to see what turns up. Scorpio and Gemini share a common characteristic— curiosity.

The idea of the ploughman is worth continuing with for a few moments longer. The ploughman isn't ploughing the field to turn up the worms for the birds—he has another purpose in mind, and his ploughing is a necessary preamble to that. So, too, the Scorpio does his investigation and his analysis as necessary groundwork for his larger ambitions, but the Gemini is interested in what he turns up anyway. The larger ambitions are not of the slightest concern to him.

Gemini is the great assimilator of trivia. His energy is almost entirely mental, and is so concentrated in the rational side of his mind that he leaves almost no emotional shadows at all, which makes him almost invisible to you. Remember that you only see people through their emotional responses; Gemini responds intellectually and verbally to his circumstances, not emotionally. How you would like to have his mind! What a waste, it seems to you, to have so fine an instrument at your command and use it to collect trivia and to make witty remarks!

You are clever and devious, you know that, but Gemini makes you feel ponderous and dull. He is so much faster than you, so quick to see the different sides of things, and you wish you could match him. He even has the capability to throw away his best ideas as though they didn't matter; you keep all of yours because they were so costly to produce. It is because he never takes anything seriously; the novelty of an idea is worth more to him than its content, and novelty cannot be kept.

He sees you as somebody with the strength to finish the job. One of his own great failings, and he knows it, is his inability to stay doing one thing for a long time. Somehow he can't raise the enthusiasm. You, however, are thoroughgoing, purposive, and successful. He can see that—and he likes it. He will never understand your need for emotional restraint, but then he doesn't deal in emotions anyway, except as an abstract concept, and he will never understand why you take things so seriously. What he does know is that his own energies are entirely mental ones, and that he lacks the forceful application that brings lasting results; your energies are primarily mental, too, and you have exactly the forceful application he needs. You are just what he needs.

A business partnership between you would be very productive indeed, because you can each contribute what the other partner particularly lacks. With your force added to his incisiveness, you could really get somewhere. Marriage would be similar, though you would have to allow for his need for movement, and realize that an attempt to dominate and dictate his behaviour would result in both of you adopting a policy of deception and subterfuge.

As lovers, you are ill matched, because his needs are for playful teasing and mental rapport, whereas yours are deeper, and both more physical and more emotional. It's like matching a rapier against a cannon—they are weapons so different that no engagement is possible. It is far better to stay as friends, and let your shared passion for finding things out amuse you both.

Scorpio-Cancer

This is the first of the partnerships within your own element, Water. There are a great many similarities between you, just as there are between the two animals that represent you in the sky. Both of you have hard shells to symbolize how your true selves are not on show to the world at large, but must be protected against attack; and both of you have pincers with which to defend yourselves against those who get too close without being invited.

What must strike you very forcibly about a Cancerian is how very private they are. They are polite enough, but it really isn't possible to see what they are thinking from the outside. You will understand this without any trouble, but you might like to remember that this is how others see you, to a great extent. An interesting thought, isn't it?

The pair of you live in a personal and internal universe where emotions and feelings are the things that matter most. In the early stages of the relationship, you will edge round each other cautiously, trying to get some idea of how the other one works without exposing yourself to possible attack. Both of you like to be quite sure of how the other person behaves before making any kind of firm commitment.

You see the Cancerian as someone with a special talent, which you would dearly like to have: they can generate emotion. They are capable of giving themselves to, and caring for, another person without first asking themselves what they are going to get out of it, and what it will cost them in time and effort. You can't do that. On the one hand, you can dismiss it as sentimental weakness, but you know that you are lying to yourself; this is real care that we are talking about, the stuff that is like gold dust to you, and the Cancerian ability to create it from inside themselves is something you find inexpressibly moving. There are dark mysteries within you somewhere, so deep that you can only just glimpse them yourself, and they have to do with the meaning of your existence. Somehow Cancer seems to have mastered them in a way that you have not. They are clearer, softer people who can manage to exist without the strong harness of self-control that you have had to wear for as long as you can remember. You feel clever and powerful most of the time; in their presence, you feel almost ashamed of yourself.

They see you as unbelievably powerful and successful individuals whose willpower borders on the manic in comparison to their own. They know that they are not always as effective as they would like to be, and their well-known sentimental streak often prevents them from being as ruthless as is sometimes necessary. It is one thing to make a lot of emotional energy, they say, but another thing altogether to direct it and make it work for you. You can do this, and they can see that. They are in awe of your ability to direct your energies towards a specific goal with enough force to make it bend to your will. In terms of the Water element that you both represent, you are a high-pressure hose, while they merely rain softly over things. They would gladly trade some of their sensitivity for some of your intensity.

This is an easy friendship to form; you both find things in the other to admire, and in communicating that you find that you work in similar ways: what you have in common, added to what you find desirable in them, draws you together. It is a fine friendship, too; you respect each other's privacy instinctively, and so avoid the vicious circle of suspicion and withdrawal that would otherwise come into being. If the friendship develops into a sexual liaison, then you should find it deeply satisfying, with many of the needs you didn't know you had being met by the understanding of someone from the same element as yourself. It will be passionate, but it needn't necessarily be energetic.

As a business partnership this one lacks the pioneering spirit to some extent, and so might not be as successful as you would think. As a marriage, it would be a much better proposition. You would have to make sure that you developed an adequate means of expression for your differences, though; jealousies and slow rages are all too easy to generate from an overabundance of the Water element.

Scorpio-Leo
This one will either work or it won't, and you'll soon know which one it is. This elemental mix is Fire and Water, both of you Fixed, and therefore impossible to overcome. The result, of course, is steam, but it remains to be seen if that can be put to any useful purpose.

The essence of this is that one of you wants to be in command, and the other wants to be in control. There is a difference between the two: you get a commander's hat if you are in command, and unless the Leo gets to wear it, he won't play.

In many ways a Leo leaves you breathless with disbelief, but you cannot help but admire him, because he seems to be able to achieve without apparent effort all the things for which you work so hard. He is a natural winner; everybody looks to him as the leader of any group, and to be in his company is generally regarded as an enjoyable experience. He radiates warmth and energy without wanting anything in return; he is genuinely generous, and it is probably this, more than anything else, which makes you suspicious. Water signs never understand that warmth radiates outwards naturally, and that Fire signs have it to spare. Indeed, if they didn't do something with it, they would probably be ill. Aries and Sagittarius put that energy into movement, but Leo prefers to sit still and radiate.

He represents what you are aiming for. What you really want is to be as popular, as liked, and to have the same regal status the Leo. What you find so amazing is that he can be so open, so self-centred, and so lazy with it. Have you not spent valuable years of your time making sure that you do everything in the most effective way? How can he be so careless, so ignorant of anything except himself, and still be where he is? Because he gives energy out, and you take it in, that's why. The world loves a giver, especially when it's all for free. At the end of the day, you can find plenty about him to despise, but you love him just the same, and you'd love to be in his shoes, just like everybody else.

He sees you as somebody with the same sort of inexhaustible power as himself. He also sees that yours is restricted, and controlled, by your own effort of will. He is attracted to somebody who is as powerful as he is, and recognizes you as a sort of earlier version of himself, someone who lacks the confidence to let loose the power inside himself. He is intrigued, interested, and a little irritated by how you try to organize him, restrict him, control him. What he doesn't want is for you to be able to contain his light, to soak him up, as it were, and he will turn his light up even brighter if he thinks this is happening, while you run for cover. He needs to be the one in command, the one that people look to, and he will fight you for that role if he thinks that you are going to take it from him. What he won't do is fight you for it if he can see that it was yours in the first place; he will simply go elsewhere. If you want him, you will have to give him first place.

Really, you need him more than he needs you, and he probably knows it. Any friendship between you will develop into a power struggle in a very short time indeed, and this will still be the case if you have a sexual relationship. In fact, it will be even more so, because the two of you represent the fundamental forces of life and death in the zodiac, so your power games are played on a cosmic level as well as an individual one. If you lose, you die; if you win, you *both* die.

If there is some interest outside the pair of you that you are both keen on, then the combination of your energies will be very strong indeed. For this reason, you would do well in business together. Privately, however, you would be fighting for power in the home, which would make for a marriage lived at a fairly high volume, with flying crockery from time to time. It really depends on how much you like a good fight. You hurt yourself each time you hurt him, you know; is this what the sting in your tail is for?

Scorpio-Virgo

Most of the relationships between signs which are two signs apart are quite amicable, but this one is really special. There aren't many people in the zodiac whose company you really enjoy, but Virgo is one. The funny thing about it is that it's the very *un*emotional qualities of the sign that you like best; the thing that you really appreciate about the Virgoans is their no-nonsense attitudes to life.

Virgos like getting things right. They approach things in a practical way. They analyse their own approach, and decide on the best way to tackle the problem. When they get down to work, they work in a structured, methodical way, and they get things right. They waste nothing, and when it's all over, the result is neat and clean. You like this sort of thing. It's almost good enough to sit and watch, but even better is the knowledge that you can rely on them to do things properly in your absence. Somebody who does things to your standards, even when you are as obsessive as you are, Scorpio, is the sort of person you would like as your friend, and it is this shared attitude of perfectionism that attracts you to each other. It is true that you do it for slightly different reasons, but the effect is the same, and that's what you recognize in each other.

It will surprise you, when you get to know a Virgo, that they are only too willing to do things for you. It will also surprise you that they do things for the sheer pleasure of doing them and getting them right—much like a child at school who likes getting ten out of ten but doesn't care much about Mathematics itself one way or the other. This makes them undemanding friends, and good ones from your point of view, because the emotional motives that underlie all your actions are never examined by them; indeed, it seldom occurs to them that such motives even exist, which suits you admirably.

They see you as exciting larger versions of themselves, dealing with big projects with the same correct and effective procedures that they use on a smaller scale. They like your attitude: or, to be more accurate, they like your apparent attitude. Your true motives are beyond them—they live in a world of material and practical details, where the emotional content of things is almost non-existent, and where human hopes and fears are dismissed as unreliable and uninteresting.

A friendship between you is most likely to start as a working partnership, and it works brilliantly on that level. They are likely to be the most enthusiastic and reliable helpmates you will ever find, knowing instinctively how you would like to about things, and gaining as much satisfaction as you do when things go according to plan.

It is probably a mistake to attempt a sexual relationship with a Virgo. They are completely unfamiliar with your Martian energy, both in its quality and its intensity, and you will overwhelm them. At the same time, you will be irritated by their inability to respond to, or even understand, the strength of your emotional needs.

As a business partnership, things will go well. It is absolutely imperative that you are in the leading position, so that they are working for you rather than with you, in effect, but you are likely to arrange it that way anyway, so there should be no problems. A Virgoan isn't really happy leading the way, and will voice no protest if you take the driving seat.

Marriage is probably not a good idea, despite the fact that you work so well together. They will never come to terms with the intensity of your emotion, and you will wear them down after a while. They do *worry* so when they are unsure of themselves, and you will in fact make them ill after a little while. Keep them as friends and helpmates, and leave it at that.

Scorpio-Libra

This one gets a maximum difficulty rating, if such a thing exists for a relationship. You are different in element, quality, and just about everything else that there is; in addition, they are the sign behind you in the zodiac, and so embody all the qualities that you would rather not think about, or feel that you have outgrown. Despite all that, though, the relationship seems determined to form itself, whether you want it or not. It just happens that way—there is an attraction between you.

The attraction is the easiest thing to explain. Libra is one of Venus' signs, and you, of course, are one of Mars'. These two planets seem to have a magnetic effect on each other, or at least on the people who display their energies, such that they find themselves propelled towards each other. Librans are always looking for a partnership to form, and they have a very romantic view of life; they can be attracted to anybody, and if that person makes the right sort of response, they will form a partnership. You, of course, respond to them as you respond to everybody else, with a concentrated blast of emotional power. They read this, as everybody else does, as sexual energy, and take it as a favourable response. In this way the Libran falls victim to his own capacity for attraction; he finds himself hopelessly attracted to you. You may find this amusing, but if you are busy, you might not.

You see Librans as rather pathetic figures, but at the same time rather discomfiting. They are much less sure of their purpose than you, and you see this indecisiveness as an annoying weakness. Not only do they have no idea what they are aiming for from one week to the next, but they are likely to be holding a completely different opinion about things from one week to the next, and if you like things to stay more or less constant (as you do), that's annoying. They have a knack for saying the right thing, for putting people at their ease; they are friendly to everybody, and everybody has them as a friend. You see this as a useful talent, but when you look a little closer you are surprised at how shallow the content of their conversation really is. Why waste a talent for dealing with people so well, you think to yourself, by keeping it to so trivial a level? You can't understand that the Libran is being nice for its own sake: there is no ulterior motive.

You are actually made uneasy by their apparent happiness, the more so because you cannot understand where it comes from. Can they really have no purpose other than to make friends with everyone? Where does their energy come from? How can they afford to be so open and welcoming to everybody the whole time? The answer is actually very obvious, but you are unlikely to see it, and when you know what it is, you will be even more upset. It is simply this: they are happy to share things.

Sharing is the *last* thing you would think of. It is completely alien to the way that you work. What's worse, you know that it makes a sort of sense, but you'd rather not be reminded of that. Now you see why the relationship won't work unless you are prepared to make a special effort: how can you be happy with a person whose definition of happiness is the very thing you would most like to avoid?

Libra does not have this trouble. He is simply besotted with you, and you can do with him as you wish. He is helpless in your hands.

A friendship between you will last only for a few minutes before Venus and Mars, acting through you, make you decide to become lovers. In this area, the energies are most unevenly matched: Libra will be expecting something loving and romantic—your powerful passions and concentrated power will completely stagger him. From your point of view, his inability to match you with similar strength to your own will leave you unsatisfied.

As a marriage, or as business partners, this pairing would probably take more than it was worth to make it work properly. If, but only if, you were prepared to change yourself, become more flexible and less obsessive, and if the Libran were particularly strong-willed and creative, then you might make a marriage with something to it—but you might not.

Scorpio-Scorpio
At least you know what you're getting here. Have a look in a mirror. Make a fist. Do you notice how the mirror image makes a fist from his other hand to oppose you exactly? That's what this relationship is going to be like.

Some signs go rather better with themselves than others, because of the accommodating nature of the signs themselves. Scorpios don't qualify on that count.

The trouble, of course, is that you both want to be in control, and neither of you is prepared to give way. You are frightened that as you find out more about him, he is busy finding out the same sort of things about you. You will attempt to find his weaknesses, and when you have done that, you will feel a lot more sure of yourself. He may also have found yours, and you may not be aware of it. He may have deceived you as to his. There are all sorts of possibilities. The pair of you may actually enjoy this game of secrets a lot more than you are prepared to admit; if so, all well and good, especially if it takes place within, say, a sexual framework. If it becomes at all serious, really seriously serious as opposed to ordinarily serious (Scorpios have a wide range of seriousness), then you will be in danger of destroying each other for ever. The venom in the scorpion's sting is not for pretend battles.

You are both very possessive. This possessiveness extends out beyond the individual to cover a vast territory of people and experience, all of whom you regard as your exclusive property.

You do think that you own them in a material sense, but you are sure that you control them, and that their every movement is ultimately referred back to you. This wide sphere of influence is your own special world, and if it overlaps with that of another Scorpio, then one of you must be mistaken: if you control that bit, then they can't, can they? The idea of being mistaken is one which you do walking backwards if you are not to turn your back on your adversary, and scorpions, like crabs, walk sideways or forwards.

The way out of this constant feuding is quite simple. Go back and look in the mirror again. Now turn to face right. Take a step. You are both walking in the same direction.

You will need a common goal large enough and far enough into the future to occupy the pair of you. If possible, it will need to have different facets, so that one of you would like to control one side of it, and the other another. You can both use your considerable organizational talents to attack this target, and you can help each other up through the structure of the thing so that eventually you both stand at the top. It is the only way; you both need a purpose, and you both like being busy, and the feeling that you are getting somewhere. You must simply ensure that in helping yourselves you are helping each other, and that you do not trespass on each other's chosen territory as you do it.

All very easy in theory, but not quite so simple in practice. As your working partnership flourishes, your day-to-day friendship will look after itself, though it may come to be inward-looking, and to discourage outsiders from joining in.

As lovers, you will have to be very sure of your own territory again. With confidence and a feeling of mutual trust will come the ability to let go some of that awesome Martian force at full strength at each other, and you will enjoy that very much; but if anything undermines that confidence and trust, then the imbalance in the relationship will have disastrous consequences. You must be particularly wary of giving any cause for jealousy. It's quite simple, really: if you are going to work with high voltage, observe the safety regulations.

As a marriage? Yes: very powerful, very private, very successful, *if* you can maintain each other's total trust and confidence.

Scorpio-Sagittarius

Sagittarians are wonderful people. They will remind you of this fact, using those very words, whenever they feel that you need a reminder. Their arrogance makes you cringe at times, but they seem to get away with it, and you find them very attractive. They don't find you anything like so enticing though, and a lasting relationship between you is a hard thing to achieve.

You spend a lot of your time finding out about things. Background information, mainly; how things are, how they got that way, who does what, that sort of thing. You do this so that you will have an effective plan of action and a sure chance of success. Sagittarians are better than that. They know everything already; it comes built-in, somehow. They also know how people are going to move, because they are perceptive that way. And they are successful because they have energy, talent, and luck. It makes you sick.

You see them as having all the knowledge that you would ever like to have, but they appear to give it out to everybody and anybody, for free. If it were yours, your reason, you would put it to some good purpose, capitalizing on the advantage it gave you. That's fixed-sign thinking. Sagittarius is mutable; he spends his time doing things for other people, giving his talent away. He is also Fire where you are Water, so if he doesn't parade his talent and show off a little he will become ill. Energy is indeed free, to him anyway, and he does not have to collect it the way you do. He is more than happy to offload some of it in your direction, and this suits you fine for a short while, but he will begin to wonder what you do with it all.

Energy and friendliness, according to him, are for spreading around and giving out; it isn't fair for somebody to attempt to control it all. He has an almost childish sense of honesty and fair play, and he will tell you off if you attempt to take more than he thinks is your fair share. He will also resent your attempts to contain his movements; he needs to be on the move all the time, seeing new things.

He sees you as an inverted version of himself. He appreciates your inquiring mind, and admires your effective way of working; he also recognizes something similar to his own enthusiasm in your intense dedication to your own interests. What he doesn't like, though, is the way that your world is inward-facing; he is sure that you are missing the point somehow, and that knowledge and talents are to be shared. He doesn't care for money in the same way that you do, either: as far as he's concerned it is only useful when spent, whereas you can appreciate the power it has for its own sake. Power of any kind doesn't interest him—knowledge does. You can understand that, you think. Not so: you understand the power of knowledge, but he has the joy of knowledge.

Since he can offer you more than you can offer him, the friendship will be one-sided. He is quite willing to be friends with you, but only for as long as it interests him; if you are interesting, different, and communicative, then you will gain his attention, but not otherwise. You will have to work very hard indeed: how you do captivate somebody you are desperate to know, but who doesn't want what you've got? Once you get talking, you will be surprised how easy it can be: Sagittarians talk about almost anything. They will talk about grand concepts and universal deals rather than personal and individual matters, and you will find that you know more about this sort of thing than you perhaps thought. You will certainly make bright company for each other, or at least until the Sagittarian fancies a change!

As a lover, you will find him strong and imaginative, but playful in a way that upsets you; he will refuse to take the affair as seriously as you do, and you may get the feeling that he is thinking about something else some of the time. This leads to Scorpionic jealousy, and is, of course, detrimental to the situation.

As marriage partners, you would have to make some major adjustments. You would have to live with his changeability, and he would have to realize how little you like moving unless you really have to. He would accuse you of not being honest with him, and you would accuse him of not taking the situation seriously enough. It could all work out very well, but the odds are very much against it, as they are against a successful business partnership, too.

Scorpio-Capricorn

This is the one you have been waiting for. Capricorns like Scorpios, and Scorpios like Capricorns. This is quite possibly the easiest and best suited combination of signs in the whole zodiac, and the two of you just can't help but get on with each other. What's more, you can actually do something positive for each other, which pleases you both a great deal.

Capricorn is the cardinal Earth sign. What a Capricorn likes to see is a structured approach to life; to him, everything has a framework to fit into, and a set of rules. He likes to play by the rules, and he likes to succeed. What he likes best of all is the recognition he gets for his position, and the status it brings him. A man after your own heart, as you can see.

The difference between you is that Capricorn is very unemotional. Quite cold, in fact. He is not interested in the emotional side of things, and he doesn't trust people who are; to him, such people are unreliable and ineffective, not firm enough. He likes you, though: he sees your intense Martian energy, and the way you pursue your objectives, and he is impressed. Your emotional objectives are hidden from him, and very successfully.

Because he is an Earth sign, Capricorn values material possessions. He uses these possessions and his status in his career as the yardsticks for his existence. The harder he works, the more money he has, and the higher he rises. As he goes up the ladder of success, he acquires larger cars and larger houses. Each of these represents the amount of work necessary to acquire them, in his eyes. What he is doing, in fact, is converting effort into material form, and everybody accords him respect and status according to the size and quantity of his status symbols. This is a very interesting process to you; you want to be a success too, and you want people to recognize you as somebody with obvious power. They way to do this is with material tokens, similar to the ones a Capricorn uses, but you are not really able to do this on your own, because you are a Water sign; Capricorn can help.

He sees you as a tremendous source of concentrated energy. He is a hard worker himself, but he has to do it with patient toil over many years, because his ruling planet, Saturn, has none of the immediate heat and force that your planet, Mars, has. Quite often he gets very tired; he knows that he has to press on, and he knows where he wants to be at the end of it all, but it takes a lot out of him, and it takes a long time. When he sees your talent for concentrated activity and organized control he sighs with envy. It's exactly the sort of thing he would wish for if he had three wishes (except that he's too down-to-earth to believe in fairies).

What makes you such firm friends so quickly is mutual approval. You are both likely to find the other visually attractive, since you both dress in a way that suggests a businesslike approach. As you get to know each other, you encourage each other to talk about plans and projects, and voice your approval of the other's approach. With the Capricorn's perception of structures, and capacity for long-term effort linked to your sense of purpose and ability to discern motives, you will make a formidable business partnership which will bring you greater rewards than either of you could achieve on your own.

As an intimate relationship this combination suffers a little from being too regimented and goal-oriented. As a marriage it would be very successful in terms of your careers and material success, but it lacks warmth and the ability to comfort itself in times of trouble. Sexually, you find the Capricorn a bit of a puzzle; they are strong and potent like the goats of their sign, but they don't have *passion*; depth of feeling just isn't in them.

Scorpio-Aquarius

The last of the Fixed signs. There is a lot that you two have in common; or, to be more accurate, you indulge in similar behaviour for different reasons, and you can recognize it in each other. The essential idea is one of remoteness, of keeping yourself to yourself.

Aquarians are funny creatures. You will not be able to notice anything unusual about them at first, because they don't do anything that sticks in your memory. Your particular memory, remember, works with the emotional responses and motivations of those around you, and an Aquarian is an Air sign, so he is emotionally rather cool. He is also ruled by Saturn, the coldest planet astrologically, so you can't expect him to generate a lot of emotional heat for you to pick up.

Aquarians are sociable. So sociable, in fact, that you will seldom find one on his own. In a group of people he really comes to life, somehow taking on all the characteristics of the group as a whole. What he likes doing is meeting lots of new people, and being in company. He's not too keen on personal and intimate relationships, because in them the emotional temperature tends to rise, and he'd rather be cool; larger groups are where he's at home.

The interesting thing about all this socializing is that although he is very much part of the group, he keeps himself aloof within it, as though he was watching a play unfold around him. He is interested and amused, but he is not really committed to the hopes and fears of any of the individuals in his group. He is polite and friendly, and he likes his surroundings to be full of friendly people, but his best friend is still himself. The thing he feels most strongly for, actually, are ideas which affect a whole group of people, such as a political opinion, or a protest movement. He is dedicated to being friends with everyone, and that means that everyone has to be on the same level as he is; he is firmly opposed to all kinds of hierarchy, and any system which gives one person more power than another. Nobody has power over him, he thinks; he is unique, special, independent, and his own man.

You can recognize in him the idea of keeping your own thoughts to yourself while appearing to be an active member of a group—it's the sort of thing you do all the time. You're not so keen on his egalitarian ideals, though; to you, power is one of your main aims. He is, of course, the outgoing part of the cycle of which you are the incoming: what he is doing is putting his energies out into a large group of people, and you collect it back in again. Both of you need large numbers of people to function effectively, and you both keep yourselves effectively one step back from the people you spend your time with.

In you he sees the principle of emotional control taken to its highest form. He doesn't like your love of power, but he likes your ability to analyse and gauge any situation, because it is a similar process to the one he uses. What he would perhaps like to have is your passionate belief in yourself and your own purpose; Saturn doesn't give him as much heat as other people have, and he finds that attractive.

It is surprising that the two of you talk to each other at all; you may just be too remote ever to risk communicating. Assuming you do, the friendship will be firm but cool; you realize how necessary the other is to your own activities in the long run, you appreciate your similarities, but you don't feel the necessity to talk about it all the time. It's an instinctive thing.

As business partners you are too far apart in your basic principles to make much progress, but as marriage partners you could well be better suited than people would have you believe: you wouldn't get in each other's way, but the Aquarian would appreciate some of your Martian heat. Sexually you will find him cool, but strong and inventive; from time to time he will really surprise you.

Scorpio-Pisces

Some of these relationships are good for your career, and some have been good for your physical well-being; this one is good for your soul. Pisces is the last of the Water signs, and the most fluid of them all. Completely unstructured and infinitely flexible, he represents the ultimate challenge to your ideas about yourself.

Pisces lives entirely in his imagination. Like the two fishes of his symbol, he lives in the emotional world of the Water element, and often seems to swim in two directions at once. Self control isn't important to him, as it is to you; instead, he lets his emotions flow wherever he wants, and forms his reality out of them. He is completely caught up in whatever he is feeling at the time, and his version of the truth is formed from the feelings he is experiencing at any given moment.

The randomness of this horrifies you. You want to tell them to get hold of some sort of plan, some set of rules, so that they can at least be consistent in themselves, and then to impose some sort of order on their surroundings. Their whole existence seems so disturbingly loose.

They are not likely to be impressed by the argument. For a Piscean, the essence of life is to feel the force of emotion, to be carried along by the experience. Even if the emotion is a bad one, there's no need to worry, another one will be along in a minute. There is, of course, the awful thought that the world might run out of emotional energy, but luckily there are people like you around to store it up and keep the flow going with your intensity and passion.

You are, of course, worrying for nothing; if you let your emotions go, as they do, you would soon find that the tremendous pressure subsided almost as soon as it was released, giving a gentle flow for you to swim around in. The Piscean is the next stage in your emotional development—after you have learned self-control, and have gained the confidence never to doubt your own identity, you can allow yourself to let go a little, and see where it gets you. Your problem is that you don't actually have that confidence.

As you can see, on a day-to-day level the Piscean is so different from you that you can have hardly anything in common; it is only on a life-long level that you can see how they are one step ahead of you. Still, life is lived on a day-to-day level, and that's where relationships are formed. As a friendship, these two signs get on very well—rather better than you would like. Let me explain. Pisces will take the form of anything which his companion wants him to be, so if you are going to be forceful and dominant, they will respond in a similar manner, which you will find most encouraging. What you won't find encouraging is that they will instinctively know what you *really* mean, because they are almost psychically sensitive; it is no use at all being devious with them, because they can perceive your real meaning at once. It is no use trying to control them, either; water runs through your fingers, you know.

If you want to extend this shadow-boxing into your love life, you will find that they are a lot more subtle and sensitive than you had at first supposed; they are capable of matching your emotional strength when it suits them, but you can't match their changes of temperament.

You would find them difficult business partners, unless you defined the rules very closely indeed; their mutability means that they will frequently modify their way of working as it suits them, and that would infuriate you. Marriage would be rather better; there the private side of your life needs to be developed as well as the public side, and what they have to teach you about the development of your Watery energies would be beneficial in the long run.

Part 3

Your Life

5. The Year within Each Day

You have probably wondered, in odd moments, why there are more than twelve varieties of people. You know more than twelve people who look completely different. You also know more than one person with the same Sun sign as yourself who doesn't look anything like you. You also know two people who look quite like each other, but who are not related, and do not have birthdays near each other, so can't be of the same Sun sign. You will have come to the conclusion that Sun signs and astrology don't work too well, because anyone can see that there are more than twelve sorts of people.

You will also have wondered, as you finished reading a newspaper or magazine horoscope, how those few sentences manage to apply to a twelfth of the nation, and why it is that they are sometimes very close to your true circumstances, and yet at other times miles off. You will have come to the conclusion that astrology isn't all that it might be, but some of it is, and that you like it enough to buy magazines for the horoscopes, and little books like this one.

It might be that there is some other astrological factor, or factors, which account for all the different faces that people have, the similarities between people of different Sun signs, and the apparent inconsistencies in magazine horoscopes. There are, indeed, lots of other astrological factors we could consider, but one in particular will answer most of the inconsistencies we have noticed so far.

It is the Ascendant, or rising sign. Once you know your
Ascendant, you will see how you get your appearance, your way
of working, your tastes, your preferences and dislikes, and your
state of health (or not, as the case may be). It is perhaps of more
use to you to consider yourself as belonging to your Ascendant
sign, than your Sun sign. You have been reading the wrong
newspaper horoscopes for years; you are not who you thought
you were!

You are about to protest that you know when your birthday is.
I'm sure you do. This system is not primarily linked to your
birthday, though. It is a smaller cogwheel in the clockwork of the
heavens, and we must come down one level from where we have
been standing to see its movements. Since astrology is basically
the large patterns of the sky made small in an individual, there
are a number of 'step-down' processes where the celestial
machinery adjusts itself to the smaller scale of mankind; this is
one of them.

Here's the theory:

Your birthday pinpoints a particular time during the year. The
Sun appears to move round the strip of sky known as the zodiac
during the course of the year. In reality, of course, our planet
Earth, moves round the Sun once a year, but the great friendly
feature of astrology is that it always looks at things from our
point of view; so, we think we stand still, and the Sun appears to
move through the zodiac. On a particular day of importance
such as your birthday, you can see which of the zodiac signs the
Sun is in, pinpoint how far it has gone in its annual trip round the
sky, and then say 'This day is important to me, because it is my
birthday; therefore this part of the sky is important to me
because the Sun is there on my special day. What are the
qualities of that part of the Sun's journey through the zodiac
and what are they when related to me?' The answer is what you
usually get in a horoscope book describing your Sun sign.

Fine. Now let's go down one level, and get some more detail.
The Earth rotates on its own axis every day. This means that
from our point of view, we stand still and the sky goes round us
once a day. Perhaps you hadn't thought of it before, but that's

how the Sun appears to move up and across the sky from sunrise to sunset. It's actually us who are moving, but we see it the other way round. During any day, then, your birthday included, the whole of the sky goes past you at some time or another; but at a particular moment of importance, such as the time that you were born, you can see where the Sun is, see which way up the sky is, and say, 'This moment is important to me, because I was born at this time; therefore the layout of the sky has the same qualities as I do. What are the qualities of the sky at this time of day, and what are they when related to me?'

You can see how you are asking the same questions one level lower down. The problem is that you don't know which bit of the sky is significant. Which bit do you look at? All you can see? All that you can't (it's spherical from your point of view, and has no joins; half of it is below the horizon, remember)?

How about directly overhead? A very good try; the point in the zodiac you would arrive at is indeed significant, and is used a lot by astrologers, but there is another one which is more useful still. The eastern horizon is the point used most. Why? Because it fulfils more functions than any other point. It gives a starting point which is easily measurable, and is even visible (remember, all astrology started from observations made before mathematics or telescopes). It is also the contact point between the sky and the earth, from our point of view, and thus symbolizes the relationship between the sky and mankind on the earth. Finally, it links the smaller cycle of the day to the larger one of the year, because the Sun starts its journey on the eastern horizon each day as it rises; and, if we are concerned with a special moment, such as the time of your birth, then the start of the day, or the place that it started, at any rate, is analogous to the start of your life. Remember that you live the qualities of the moment you were born for all of your life; you are that moment made animate.

The point in the zodiac, then, which was crossing the eastern horizon at the time you were born, is called the Ascendant. If this happened to be somewhere in the middle of Gemini, then you have a Gemini Ascendant, or Gemini rising, whichever phrase you prefer. You will see that this has nothing to do with the time

Handwritten calculations:

$$\frac{33}{365} \times 100 \qquad 365\overline{)3300}$$

365
730
109 5
460

STAR TIME (HOURS) — chart of zodiac signs on the horizon at different times for GLASGOW, MAN-CHESTER, and LONDON:

Row	Signs across the star-time scale (0–23 hours)
GLASGOW	LEO · VIRGO · LIBRA · SCORPIO · SAGITTARIUS · CAPRICORN · AQUARIUS · PISCES · ARIES · TAURUS · GEMINI · CANCER · LEO
MANCHESTER	LEO · VIRGO · LIBRA · SCORPIO · SAGITTARIUS · CAPRICORN · AQUARIUS · PISCES · ARIES · TAURUS · GEMINI · CANCER
LONDON	CANCER · LEO · VIRGO · LIBRA · SCORPIO · SAGITTARIUS · CAPRICORN · AQUARIUS · PISCES · ARIES · TAURUS · GEMINI · CANCER

Different signs are on the horizon at different times according to where you live, as you can see. This is because of the difference in latitude. If you live in between the places given, you can make a guess from the values here. To compensate for longitude, subtract twelve minutes from your birthtime if you live in Glasgow, Liverpool or Cardiff; ten minutes for Edinburgh or Manchester, and six minutes for Leeds, Tyneside, or the West Midlands. *Add* four minutes for Norwich.

of year that you were born, only with the time of day.

Have a look at the diagrams on page 72, which should help explain things. If two people are born on the same day, but at different times, then the Ascendant will be different, and the Sun and all the other planets will be occupying different parts of the sky. It makes sense to assume, then, that they will be different in a number of ways. Their lives will be different, and they will look different. What they will have in common is the force of the Sun in the same sign, but it will show itself in different ways because of the difference in time and position in the sky.

How do you know which sign was rising over the eastern horizon when you were born? You will have to work it out. In the past, the calculation of the Ascendant has been the subject of much fuss and secrecy, which astrologers exploit to the full, claiming that only they can calculate such things. It does take some doing, it is true, but with a few short cuts and a calculator it need only take five minutes.

Here is the simplest routine ever devised for you to calculate your own Ascendant, provided that you know your time of birth. Pencil your answers alongside the stages as you go, so you know where you are.

1. Count forwards from 23 October to your birthday: 23 October is 1, 24 October is 2, and so on.
   Total days: . . . .

2. Add 31 to this. New total is: . . . .

3. Divide by 365, and then

4. Multiply by 24. Answer is now: . . . .
   (Your answer by now is between 0 and 24. If it isn't, you have made a mistake somewhere. Go back and try again.)

5. Add your time of birth, in 24-hour clock time. If you were born at 3 p.m., that means 15. If you were born in Summer Time, take one hour off. If there are some spare minutes, your calculator would probably like them in decimals, so it's 0.1 of an hour for each six minutes. 5.36 p.m. is 17.6, for example. Try to be as close as you can. New total is: . . . . *13·02·17·*

                                              15·17·

6. If your total exceeds 24, subtract 24. Your answer must now be between 0 and 24. Answer is: . . . .

7. You have now got the time of your birth not in clock time, but in sidereal, or star, time, which is what astrologers work in. Page 72 has a strip diagram with the signs of the zodiac arranged against a strip with the values 0 to 24, which are hours in star time. Look against the time you have just calculated, and you will see which sign was rising at the time you were born. For example, if your calculated answer is 10.456, then your Ascendant is about the 16th degree of Scorpio.

What Does the Ascendant Do?

Broadly speaking, the Ascendant does two things. Firstly, it gives you a handle on the sky, so that you know which way up it was at the time you entered the game, so to speak; this has great significance later on in the book, when we look at the way you handle large areas of activity in your life such as your career, finances, and ambitions. Secondly, it describes your body. If you see your Sun sign as your mentality and way of thinking, then your Ascendant sign is your body and your way of doing things. Think of your Sun sign as the true you, but the Ascendant as the vehicle you have to drive through life. It is the only one you have, so you can only do with it the things of which it is capable, and there may be times when you would like to do things in a different way, but it 'just isn't you'. What happens over your life is that your Sun sign energies become specifically adapted to express themselves to their best via your Ascendant sign, and you become an amalgam of the two. If you didn't, you would soon become very ill. As a Scorpio with, say, a Capricorn Ascendant, you do things from a Scorpio motivation, but in a Capricornian way, using a Capricornian set of talents and abilities, and a Capricornian body. The next few sections of the book explain what this means for each of the Sun/Ascendant combinations.

Some note ought to be made of the correspondence between

the Ascendant and the actual condition of the body. Since the Ascendant sign represents your physical frame rather than the personality inside it, then the appearance and well-being of that frame is also determined by the Ascendant sign. In other words, if you have a Libra Ascendant, then you should look like a Libran, and you should be subject to illnesses in the parts of the body with a special affinity to that sign.

The Astrology of Illness

This is worth a book in itself, but it is quite important to say that the astrological view of illness is that the correlation between the individual and the larger universe is maintained. In other words, if you continue over a long period of time with a way of behaviour that denies the proper and necessary expression of your planetary energies, then the organ of your body which normally handles that kind of activity for your body systems will start to show the stresses to you. A simple example: Gemini looks after the lungs, which circulate air, and from which oxygen is taken all over the body. Gemini people need to circulate among a lot of people, talking and exchanging information. They act as the lungs of society, taking news and information everywhere. They need to do this to express their planetary energies, and society needs them to do this or it is not refreshed, and does not communicate. You need your lungs to do this, too. Lungs within people, Geminis within society: same job, different levels. If you keep a Gemini, or he keeps himself, through circumstance or ignorance, in a situation where he cannot talk or circulate, or where he feels that his normal status is denied, then he is likely to develop lung trouble. This need not be anything to do with a dusty atmosphere, or whether he smokes, although obviously neither of those will help; they are external irritants, and this is an internal problem caused by imbalance in the expression of the energies built into him since birth. In the sections which follow, all the observations on health are to do with how the body shows you that certain behaviour is unbalancing you and causing unnecessary stress; problems from these causes are alleviated by listening to yourself and changing your behaviour.

Your Ascendant

Aries Ascendant

If you have Aries rising, you are an uncommon individual, because Aries only rises for about fifty minutes out of the twenty-four hour day. You must have been born in the middle of the afternoon, or else you have got your sums wrong somewhere.

What you are trying to do with yourself is project a Scorpio personality through an Arian vehicle. You will always be trying to do things faster than anybody else, and this can lead to hastiness and a certain degree of accident-proneness. What you see as the correct way to do things involves immediate action by the most direct method, to secure instant, and measurable, results. You feel that unless you are directly and personally responsible for doing things, then they cannot be done, not only because you believe that only you can do them properly, but because you get no satisfaction from letting anybody else do anything. Personal experience of everything is the only way you learn; reading about it, or watching it, does nothing for you.

You are likely to have headaches as a recurring problem if you push yourself too hard, and you should watch your blood pressure too. Mars, ruling Aries, is a strong and forceful planet, and it is bound to get you a little over-stressed at times. You are also likely to have problems digesting things properly. Astrologically, all illnesses apply to your external condition as well as your internal condition, so think carefully; when your head aches you are banging it too hard against a problem which cannot be overcome that way, and when you are not digesting properly, you have not understood the implications of what you have taken on. In both cases, allow time to think and consider.

Taurus Ascendant

You were born at sunset if you have Taurus rising. Taureans are generally fond of food—did you arrive in time for dinner? You should have all the Taurean physical characteristics: quite thick-set, big around the neck and shoulders sometimes, and with large hands. You should have a broad mouth, and large eyes, which are very attractive. You should also have a good voice—not only as a singing voice, but one which is pleasant to listen to in conversation too.

The Taurean method for getting things done is to look forward to, and then enjoy, the material reward for one's efforts. It is part of Taurean thinking that if you can't touch it, buy it, own it or eat it, it isn't real and it isn't worth much. You will also be concerned to keep what is yours, not to waste your energies on what won't gain you anything or increase your possessions, and not to attempt anything which you don't think you have more than a chance of achieving.

Taureans do have taste; not only taste for food, which they love, but artistic taste, which they develop as a means of distinguishing things of value which they would then like to acquire and gain pleasure from owning. Unlike the Capricorn way of doing things, which values quality because it is valued by others, Taureans enjoy their possessions for themselves. The drawback to the Taurean approach is the lack of enterprise, and the unwillingness to try things just for the fun of it.

Taurean Ascendant people have throat and glandular problems, and all problems associated with being overweight. They can also have back and kidney problems caused as a result of an unwillingness to let things go in their external life. A lighter touch is needed in the approach to problems of possession; shedding unwanted or outworn things in a desirable process.

Gemini Ascendant

If you have a Gemini Ascendant you were born somewhere in the early evening. You should have expressive hands and a wide range of gestures which you use as you speak (ask your friends!) and you are perhaps a little taller than average, or than other members of your family. Gemini Ascendant people also have dark hair, if there is any possibility of it in their parents' colouring, and quick, penetrating eyes which flash with amusement and mischief; Gemini Ascendant women have very fine eyes indeed.

The Gemini approach to things, which you find yourself using, is one in which the idea of a thing is seen as being the most useful, and in which no time must be lost in telling it to other people so that they can contribute their own ideas and responses to the discussion. The performance of the deed is of no real importance in the Gemini view; somebody else can do that. Ideas and their development are what you like to spend time on, and finding more people to talk to, whose ideas can be matched to your own, seems to you to offer the most satisfaction.

There are two snags to the Gemini approach. The first is that there is a surface quality to it all, in which the rough outline suffices, but no time is spent in development or long-term experience. It may seem insignificant, but there is some value in seeing a project through to the end. The second snag is similar, but is concerned with time. The Gemini approach is immediate, in that it is concerned with the present or the near future. It is difficult for a Gemini Ascendant person to see farther than a few months into the future, if that; it is even more difficult for him to extend his view sideways in time to see the impact of his actions on a wider scene. Both of these things he will dismiss as unimportant.

Gemini Ascendant people suffer from chest and lung maladies, especially when they cannot communicate what they want to or need to, or when they cannot circulate socially in the way that they would like. They also have problems eliminating wastes from their bodies, through not realizing the importance of ending things as well as beginning them. In both cases, thinking and planning on a broader scale than usual, and examination of the past to help make better use of the future, is beneficial.

Cancer Ascendant
You were born in the late evening if you have your Ascendant in Cancer and your Sun in Scorpio. The Cancerian frame, through which you project your energies, may mean that you appear rounder and less forceful than other Scorpios. Your energies are

in no way diminished; in fact, you are likely to be even more determined to get things right. Your face could be almost cherubic, and you could have small features in a pale complexion with grey eyes and brown hair. The key to the Cancer frame is that it is paler than usual, less well defined than usual, and has no strong colouring. Strong noses and red hair do not come from a Cancerian Ascendant.

The Cancerian approach to things is highly personal. All general criticisms are taken personally, and all problems in any procedure for which they have responsibility are seen as a personal failing. You will be concerned to use your energies for the safe and secure establishment of things from the foundations up, so that you know that whatever you have been involved in has been done properly, and is unlikely to let you down in any way; you are concerned for your own safety and reputation. The other side of this approach is that you can be a little too concerned to make sure everything is done personally, and be unwilling to entrust things to other people. Not only does this overwork you, it seems obsessive and uncooperative to others.

The Cancer Ascendant person has health problems with the maintenance of the flow of fluids in his body, and a tendency to stomach ulcers caused by worry. Cancer Ascendant women should pay special attention to their breasts, since the affinity between the sign, the Moon as ruler of all things feminine, and that particular body system means that major imbalances in the life are likely to show there first. There could also be some problems with the liver and the circulation of the legs; the answer is to think that, metaphorically, you do not have to support everybody you know: they can use their own legs to stand on, and you do not have to feed them either.

Leo Ascendant
You were born around midnight if you have Leo as an Ascendant sign. Leo, as the determinant of the physical characteristics, makes itself known by the lion of the sign—you can always spot the deep chest, proud and slightly pompous way of walking, and, more often than not, the hair arranged in some sort of a mane,

either full or taken back off the face, and golden if possible. A Leo Ascendant will bring to the fore any hereditary tendency to golden colouring, so reddish or golden hair, or a rosy complexion, may be in evidence, as will a heavy build in the upper half of the body.

The Leonine way of doing things is to put yourself in the centre and work from the centre outwards, making sure that everybody knows where the commands are coming from. It is quite a tiring way of working; you need to put a lot of energy into it, because you are acting as the driving force for everybody else. Preferred situations for this technique are those where you already know, more or less, what's going to happen; this way you are unlikely to be thrown off balance by unexpected developments. The grand gesture belongs to the Leo method; it works best if all processes are converted into theatrical scenes, with roles acted rather than lived. Over-reaction, over-dramatization, and over-indulgence are common, but the approach is in essence kind-hearted and well-meant. Children enjoy being with Leo Ascendant people, and they enjoy having children around them. The flaws in the approach are only that little gets done in difficult circumstances where applause and appreciation are scarce commodities, and that little is attempted that is really new and innovatory.

The health problems of the Leo Ascendant person come from the heart, and also from the joints, which suffer from mobility problems. These both come from a lifetime of being at the centre of things and working for everybody's good, and from being too stiff and unwilling to try any change in position. The remedy, of course, is to be more flexible, and to allow your friends to repay the favours they owe you.

Virgo Ascendant

A birth in the small hours of the morning puts Virgo on the Ascendant. Physically, this should make you slim and rather long, especially in the body; even if you have broad shoulders you will still have a long waist. There is a neatness to the features, but nothing notable; hair is brown, but again nothing notable. The nose and chin are often well-defined, and the forehead is often both tall and broad; the voice can be a little shrill and lacks penetration.

The Virgoan Ascendant person does not have an approach to life; he has a *system*. He analyses everything and pays a lot of attention to the way in which he works. It is important to the person with Virgo rising not only to be effective, but to be efficient; you can always interest them in a new or better technique. They watch themselves work, as if from a distance, all the while wondering if they can do it better. They never mind repetition; in fact they quite enjoy it, because as they get more proficient they feel better about things. To you, being able to do things is everything, and unless you are given a practical outlet for your energies, you are completely ineffective. There is a willingness to help others, to be of service through being able to offer a superior technique, inherent in the Virgo way of doing things, which prevents Virgo rising people from being seen as cold and unfriendly. They appreciate their help being appreciated. The problems in the Virgo attitude are a tendency to go into things in more detail than is necessary, and to be too much concerned with the 'proper' way to do things.

People with a Virgo Ascendant are susceptible to intestinal problems and circulatory problems, and may be prone to poor sight. All of these are ways in which the body registers the stresses of being too concerned with digesting the minutiae of things which are meant to be passed through anyway, and by not getting enough social contact. The remedy is to lift your head from your workbench sometimes, admit that the act is sometimes more important than the manner of its performance, and not to take things too seriously.

Libra Ascendant

You were born before dawn if you have Libra rising; it will give you a pleasant and approachable manner which will do a great deal to hide your anxieties and prevent people thinking anything but the best of you. You should be tallish, and graceful, as all Libra Ascendant people tend to be; they have a clear complexion, and blue eyes if possible, set in an oval face with finely formed features.

The Libra Ascendant person has to go through life at a fairly relaxed pace. The sign that controls his body won't let him feel rushed or anxious; if that sort of thing looks likely, then he will slow down a little until the panic's over. There is a need to see yourself reflected in the eyes of others, and so you will form a large circle of friends. You define your own opinion of yourself through their responses to you, rather than being sure what you want, and not caring what they think.

The drawback to the Libran approach is that unless you have approval from others, you are unlikely to do anything on your own initiative, or at least you find it hard to decide on a course of action. You always want to do things in the way which will cause the least bother to anyone, and to produce an acceptable overall result; sometimes this isn't definite enough, and you need to know what you do want as well as what you don't.

The Libran Ascendant makes the body susceptible to all ailments of the kidneys and of the skin; there may also be trouble in the feet. The kidney ailments are from trying to take all the problems out of life as you go along. Sometimes it's better simply to attack a few of the obstacles and knock them flat in pure rage—and in doing so you will develop adrenaline from the adrenal glands, on top of the kidneys!

Scorpio Ascendant
You were born around sunrise if you have a Scorpio Ascendant as well as a Scorpio Sun. A Scorpio Ascendant should give you a dark and powerful look, with a solid build, though not necessarily over-muscled, Scorpio Ascendant people tend to have a very penetrating and level way of looking at others, which is often disconcerting. Any possible darkness in the colouring is usually displayed, with dark complexions and dark hair, often thick and curly, never fine.

The Scorpio Ascendant person usually does things in a controlled manner. He is not given to explosive releases of energy unless they are absolutely necessary; even then, not often. He knows, or feels (a better word, since the Scorpionic mind makes decisions as a result of knowledge gained by feeling rather than thinking), that he has plenty of energy to spare, but uses it in small and effective doses, each one suited to the requirements of the task at hand. It does not seem useful to him to put in more effort than is strictly necessary for any one activity; that extra energy could be used somewhere else. The idea that overdoing things for their own sake is sometimes fun because of the sheer exhilaration of the release of energy does not strike a responsive chord in the Scorpio body, nor even much understanding. There is, however, understanding and perception of a situation which exists at more than one level. If anything is complicated, involving many activities and many people, with much interaction and many side issues which must be considered, then the Scorpio Ascendant person sees it all and understands all of it, in its minutest detail. They feel, and understand, the responses from all of their surroundings at once, but do not necessarily feel involved with them unless they choose to make a move. When they do move, they will have the intention of transforming things, making them different to conform to their ideas of how things need to be arranged.

Scorpio Ascendant people are unable simply to possess and look after anything; they must change it and direct it their way, and this can be a disadvantage.

Scorpio illnesses are usually to do with the genital and excretory systems; problems here relate to a lifestyle in which things are thrown away when used, or sometimes rejected when there is still use in them. It may be that there is too much stress on being the founder of the new, and on organizing others; this will bring head pains, and illnesses of that order. The solution is to take on the existing situation as it is, and look after it without changing any of it.

Sagittarius Ascendant

It would have been mid-morning when you were born for you to have a Sagittarius Ascendant. If you have, you should be taller than average, with a sort of sporty, leggy look to you; you should have a long face with pronounced temples (you may be balding there if you are male), a well-coloured complexion, clear eyes, and brown hair. A Grecian nose is sometimes a feature of this physique.

The Sagittarian Ascendant gives a way of working that is based on mobility and change. This particular frame can't keep still and is much more comfortable walking than standing, more comfortable lounging or leaning than sitting formally. You tend to be in a bit of a hurry; travelling takes up a lot of your time, because you enjoy it so. It is probably true to say that you enjoy the process of driving more than whatever it is that you have to do when you get there. You probably think a lot of your car, and you are likely to have one which is more than just a machine for transport—you see it as an extension, a representation even, of yourself. People will notice how outgoing and friendly you seem to be, but they will need to know you for some time before they realize that you enjoy meeting people more than almost anything else, and you dislike being with the same companions all the time. There is a constant restlessness in you; you will feel that being static is somehow unnatural, and it worries you. You are an optimist, but can also be an opportunist, in that you see no reason to stay doing one thing for a moment longer than it interests you. The inability to stay and develop a situation or give long-term commitment to anything is the biggest failing of this sign's influence.

A person with Sagittarius rising can expect to have problems with his hips and thighs, and possibly in his arterial system; this is to do with trying to leap too far at once, in all senses. You may also have liver and digestive problems, again caused by haste on a long-term scale. The remedy is to shorten your horizons and concentrate on things nearer home.

Capricorn Ascendant

It must have been about noon when you were born for you to have a Capricorn Ascendant. A Capricorn Ascendant will also make for great success in your chosen career, whatever it is. No matter what the job is, being born around the middle of the day guarantees public prominence whether you want it or not. This sign often gives a small frame, quite compact and built to last a long time, the sort that doesn't need a lot of feeding and isn't big enough or heavy enough to break when it falls over. The face can be narrow and the features small; often the mouth points downwards at the corners, and this doesn't change even when the person smiles or laughs.

The Capricorn sees life as an ordered, dutiful struggle. There is a great deal of emphasis placed on projecting and maintaining appearances, both in the professional and the personal life; the idea of 'good reputation' is one which everybody with Capricorn rising, whatever their sun sign, recognizes at once. There is a sense of duty and commitment which the Sagittarian Ascendant simply cannot understand; here the feeling is that there are things which need doing, so you just have to set to and get them done. Capricorn Ascendant people see far forwards in time, anticipating their responsibilities for years to come, even if their Sun sign does not normally function this way; in such cases they apply themselves to one problem at a time, but can envisage a succession of such problems, one after another, going on for years.

The disadvantages of this outlook are to do with its static nature. There is often a sense of caution that borders on the paranoid, and while this is often well disguised in affluent middle-class middle age, it seems a little odd in the young. This tends to make for a critical assessment of all aspects of a new venture before embarking on it, and as a result a lot of the original impetus is lost. This makes the result less than was originally hoped in many cases, and so a cycle of disappointment and unadventurousness sets in, which is difficult to break. The Capricorn Ascendant person is often humourless, and can seem determined to remain so.

These people have trouble in their joints, and break bones from time to time, entirely as a result of being inflexible. On a small scale this can be from landing badly in an accident because the Capricorn Ascendant keeps up appearances to the very end, refusing to believe that an accident could be happening to him: on a large scale, a refusal to move with the times can lead to the collapse of an outmoded set of values when they are swept away by progress, and this breaking up of an old structure can also cripple. They can get lung troubles, too, as a result of not taking enough fresh air, or fresh ideas. The best treatment is to look after their families rather than their reputation, and to think about the difference between stability and stagnation.

Aquarius Ascendant
Having an Aquarius Ascendant means that you were born at around lunchtime. This will make you chattier than you would otherwise have been, with a strong interest in verbal communication. There is a certain clarity, not to say transparency, about the Aquarian physique. It is usually tall, fair, and well shaped, almost never small or dark. There is nothing about the face which is particularly distinctive; no noticeable colouring, shape of nose, brows, or any other feature. It is an average sort of face, cleanly formed and clear.

The person with an Aquarian Ascendant wants to be independent. Not violently so, not the sort of independence that fights its way out of wherever it feels it's been put, just different from everybody else. Aquarius gives your body the ability to do things in ways perhaps not done before; you can discover new techniques and practices for yourself, and don't need to stay in the ways you were taught. There is a willingness to branch out, to try new things; not a Scorpionic wish to make things happen the way you want, but an amused curiosity which would just like to see if things are any better done a different way. There is no need for you to convince the world that your way is best: it only needs to suit you.

Of course, an Aquarian needs to measure his difference against others, and therefore you feel better when you have a few friends around you to bounce ideas off, as well as showing them how you're doing things in a slightly different way. You function best in groups, and feel physically at ease when you're not the only person in the room. You are not necessarily the leader of the group; just a group member. Group leaders put their energy into the group, and you draw strength and support from it, so you are unlikely to be the leader, though paradoxically all groups work better for having you in them.

A handicap arising from an Aquarian Ascendant is that you are unlikely to really feel passionately involved with anything, and this may mean that unless you have support from your friends and colleagues you will be unable to muster the determination necessary to overcome really sizeable obstacles in your chosen career.

You are likely to suffer from diseases of the circulation and in your lower legs and ankles; these may reflect a life where too much time is spent trying to be independent, and not enough support is sought from others. You may also get stomach disorders and colds because you are not generating enough heat: get more involved in things and angrier about them!

Pisces Ascendant

You were born in the afternoon if you have Pisces rising. Like Aries rising, Pisces is only possible as an Ascendant for about fifty minutes, so there aren't many of you around. Pisces Ascendant people are on the small side, with a tendency to be a bit pale and fleshy. They are not very well coordinated and so walk rather clumsily, despite the fact that their feet are often large. They have large, expressive, but rather sleepy-looking eyes.

As a Scorpio with Pisces rising, you will prefer to let things come to you than go out and look for them. The Piscean Ascendant will help you escape notice when you would rather that nobody noticed you. It will enable you to play a major role behind the scene of things, without having to be in public view at all. It will also give you an even sharper perception of people's feelings than you already have—but it will also soften your resolve, so that you become more considerate, and less brutally determined to have your own way. The major problem with a Pisces Ascendant is this inability to be active rather than reactive; you would rather be reacting to outside influences than generating your own movements from within yourself.

A Piscean Ascendant gives problems with the feet and the lymphatic system; this has connections with the way you move in response to external pressures, and how you deal with things which invade your system from outside. You may also suffer from faint-heartedness—literally as well as metaphorically. The remedy is to be more definite and less influenced by opinions other than your own.

6. Three Crosses: Areas of Life that Affect Each Other

If you have already determined your Ascendant sign from page 74, and you have read 'The Meaning of the Zodiac' on page 11, you can apply that knowledge to every area of your life with revealing results. Instead of just looking at yourself, you can see how things like your career and your finances work from the unique point of view of your birth moment.

You will remember how the Ascendant defined which way up the sky was. Once you have it the right way up, then you can divide it into sectors for different areas of life, and see which zodiac signs occupy them. After that, you can interpret each sector of sky in the light of what you know about the zodiac sign which fell in it at the time that you were born.

Below there is a circular diagram of the sky, with the horizon splitting it across the middle. This is the way real horoscopes are usually drawn. In the outer circle, in the space indicated, write the name of your Ascendant sign, not your Sun sign (unless they are the same, of course. If you don't know your time of birth, and so can't work out an Ascendant, use your Sun sign). Make it overlap sectors 12 and 1, so that the degree of your Ascendant within that sign is on the eastern horizon. Now fill in the rest of the zodiac around the circle in sequence, one across each sector boundary. If you've forgotten the sequence, look at the diagram on page 16. When you've done that, draw a symbol for the Sun ☉—a circle with a point at its centre) in one of the sectors which has your Sun sign at its edge. Think about how far through the sign your Sun is; make sure that you have put it in the right sector. Whichever sector this is will be very important to you;

having the Sun there gives a bias to the whole chart, like the weight on one side of a locomotive wheel. You will feel that the activities of that sector (or house, as they are usually called) are most in keeping with your character, and you feel comfortable doing that sort of thing.

Make sure you have got your sums right. As a Scorpio born in the afternoon, you might well have Aries rising, and the Sun in the eighth house, for example.

Now is the time to examine the twelve numbered sections of your own sky, and see what there is to be found.

Angular Houses: 1, 4, 7, 10

These are the houses closest to the horizon and the vertical, reading round in zodiacal sequence. The first house is concerned with you yourself as a physical entity, your appearance, and your health. Most of this has been dealt with in the section on

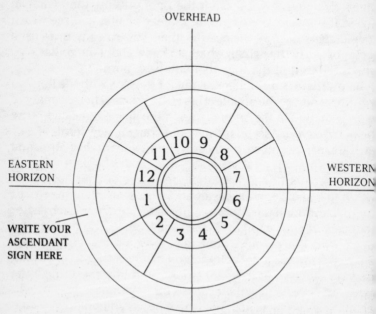

Ascendants. If you have the Sun here, it simply doubles the impact of your Sun sign energies.

Opposite to you is the seventh house, which concerns itself with everybody who is not you. Partners in a business sense, husbands, wives, enemies you are actually aware of (and who therefore stand opposed to you in plain sight) and any other unclassified strangers all belong in the seventh house. You see their motivation as being of the opposite sign to your Ascendant sign, as being something you are not. If you have Capricorn rising, you see them as behaving, and needing to be treated, which is perhaps more accurate, in a Cancerian manner. This is how you approach seventh-house things. Use the keywords from 'The Meaning of the Zodiac' (p. 17) to remind yourself what this is. If you have the Sun in the seventh house you are your own best partner: you may marry late in life, or not at all. Perhaps your marriage will be unsuccessful. It is not a failure; it is simply that you are to a very great extent self-supporting, and have neither the ability nor the need to share yourself completely with another.

The whole business of the first and the seventh is to do with me and not-me'. For the personal energies of this relationship to be shown in tangible form, it is necessary to look at the pair of houses whose axis most squarely crosses the first/seventh axis. This is the fourth/tenth. The tenth is your received status in the world, and is the actual answer to the question 'What do you take me for?' No matter what you do, the world will find it best to see you as doing the sort of thing shown by the sign in the tenth house. Eventually, you will start to pursue that kind of activity anyway, because in doing so you get more appreciation and reward from the rest of society.

Your efforts in dealing with others, which is a first/seventh thing, have their result in the tenth, and their origins in the fourth. Expect to find clues there to your family, your home, the beliefs you hold most dear, and the eventual conclusion to your life (not your death, which is a different matter). If you have the Sun in the tenth, you will achieve some measure of prominence or fame; if your Sun is in the fourth, you will do well in property, and your family will be of greater importance to you than is usual.

There is, of course, some give and take between the paired houses. Giving more time to yourself in the first house means that you are denying attention to the seventh, your partner; the reverse also applies. Giving a lot of attention to your career, in the tenth house, stops you from spending quite so much time as you might like with your family or at home. Spending too much time at home means that you are out of the public eye. There is only so much time in a day; what you give to one must be denied to the other.

This cross of four houses defines most people's lives: self, partner, home, and career. An over-emphasis on any of these is to the detriment of the other three, and all the arms of the cross feel and react to any event affecting any single member.

If these four houses have cardinal signs on them in your chart, then you are very much the sort of person who feels that he is in control of his own life, and that it is his duty to shape it into something new, personal, and original. You feel that by making decisive moves with your own circumstances you can actually change the way your life unfolds, and enjoy steering it the way you want it to go.

If these four houses have fixed signs on them in your chart, then you are the sort of person who sees the essential shape of your life as being one of looking after what you were given, continuing in the tradition, and ending up with a profit at the end of it all. Like a farmer, you see yourself as a tenant of the land you inherited, with a responsibility to hand it on in at least as good a condition as it was when you took it over. You are likely to see the main goal in all life's ups and downs as the maintenance of stability and enrichment of what you possess.

If these four houses have mutable signs on them in your chart, then you are much more willing to change yourself to suit circumstances than the other two. Rather than seeing yourself as the captain of your ship, or the trustee of the family firm, you see yourself as free to adapt to challenges as they arise, and if necessary to make fundamental changes in your life, home and career to suit the needs of the moment. You are the sort to welcome change and novelty, and you don't expect to have anything to show for it at the end of the day except experience. There is a strong sense of service in the mutable signs, and if you spend your life working for the welfare of others, then they will have something to show for it while you will not. Not in physical terms, anyway; you will have had your reward by seeing your own energies transformed into their success.

The Succedent Houses: 2, 5, 8, 11

These houses are called succedent because they succeed, or follow on from, the previous four. Where the angular houses define the framework of the life, the succedent ones give substance, and help develop it to its fullest and richest extent, in exactly the same way as fixed signs show the development and maintenance of the elemental energies defined by the cardinal signs.

The second house and the eighth define your resources; how much you have to play with, so to speak. The fifth and eleventh show what you do with it, and how much you achieve. Your immediate environment is the business of the second house. Your tastes in furniture and clothes are here (all part of your immediate environment, if you think about it) as well as your immediate resources, food and cash. Food is a resource because without it you are short of energy, and cash is a resource for obvious reasons. If you have the Sun here you are likely to be fond of spending money, and fond of eating too! You are likely to place value on things that you can buy or possess, and judge your success by your bank balance.

Opposed to it, and therefore dealing with the opposite viewpoint, is the eighth house, where you will find stored money. Savings, bank accounts, mortgages, and all kinds of non-immediate money come under this house. So do major and irreversible changes in your life, because they are the larger environment rather than the immediate one. Surgical operations and death are both in the eighth, because you are not the same person afterwards, and that is an irreversible change. If you have the Sun in the eighth you are likely to be very careful with yourself, and not the sort to expose yourself to any risk; you are also not likely to be short of a few thousand when life gets tight, because eighth house people always have some extra resource tucked away somewhere. You are also likely to benefit from legacies, which are another form of long-term wealth.

To turn all this money into some form of visible wealth you must obviously do something with it, and all forms of self-expression and ambition are found in the fifth and the eleventh houses. The fifth is where you have fun, basically; all that you like to do, all that amuses you, all your hobbies are found there, and a look at the zodiac sign falling in that house in your chart will show you what it is that you like so much. Your children are a fifth-house phenomenon, too; they are an expression of yourself made physical, made from the substance of your body and existence, and given their own. If you have the Sun in the fifth house you are likely to be of a generally happy disposition, confident that life is there to be enjoyed, and sure that something good will turn up.

The eleventh house, in contrast, is not so much what you like doing as what you would like to be doing: it deals with hopes, wishes, and ambitions. It also deals with friends and all social gatherings, because in a similar manner to the first/seventh axis, anybody who is 'not-you' and enjoying themselves must be opposed to you enjoying yourself in the fifth house. If you have the Sun in the eleventh house, you are at your best in a group. You would do well in large organizations, possibly political ones, and will find that you can organize well. You have well-defined ambitions, and know how to realize them, using other people as supporters of your cause.

The oppositions in this cross work just as effectively as the previous set did: cash is either used or stored, and to convert it from one to the other diminishes the first. Similarly, time spent enjoying yourself does nothing for your ambitions and aims, nor does it help you maintain relationships with all the groups of people you know; there again, all work and no play . . .

If you have cardinal signs on these four houses in your chart, then you think that using all the resources available to you at any one time is important. Although what you do isn't necessarily important, or even stable, you want to have something to show for it, and enjoying yourself as you go along is important to you. To you, money is for spending, and how your friends see you is possibly more important to you than how you see yourself.

Fixed signs on these four houses will make you reticent, and careful of how you express yourself. You are possibly too busy with the important things of life as you see them, such as your career and long-term prospects, to give much attention to the way you live. You feel it is important to have things of quality, because you have a long-term view of life, and you feel secure when you have some money in the bank, but you don't enjoy your possessions and friends for your own sake. You have them because you feel that you should, not because they are reason enough in themselves.

Mutable signs on these four houses show a flexible attitude to the use of a resource, possibly because the angular houses show that you already have plenty of it, and it is your duty to use it well. You don't mind spending time and money on projects which to you are necessary, and which will have a measurable and result. You see that you need to spend time and effort to bring projects into a completed reality, and you are willing to do that as long as the final product is yours and worth having. You are likely to change your style of living quite frequently during your life, and there may be ambitions which, when fulfilled, fade from your life completely.

The Cadent Houses: 3, 6, 9, 12

The final four houses are called cadent either because they fall away from the angles (horizon and vertical axes), or because they fall towards them, giving their energy towards the formation of the next phase in their existence. Either way, affairs in these houses are nothing like as firm and active as those in the other two sets of four. It may be useful to think of them as being given to mental rather than physical or material activities.

The third and ninth houses are given to thought and speech with the ninth specializing in incoming thoughts, such as reading, learning and belief (religions of all kinds are ninth house things), while the third limits itself to speaking and writing, daily chat, and the sort of conversations you have every day. If you have the Sun in the third house, you will be a chatterbox. Talking is something you could do all day, and you love reading. Anything will do—papers, magazines, novels; as long as it has words in it you will like it. You will have the sort of mind that loves accumulating trivia, but you may find that serious study or hard learning is something that you cannot do.

The third house concerns itself with daily conversation, but the ninth is more withdrawn. Study is easy for a ninth-house person, but since all ideal and theoretical thought belongs here the down-to-earth street-corner reality of the third house doesn't, and so the higher knowledge of the ninth finds no application in daily life. The third-ninth axis is the difference between practical street experience and the refined learning of a university. To give time to one must mean taking time from the other. If you have the Sun in the ninth, you are likely to have a very sure grasp of the theory of things, and could well be an instigator or director of large projects; but you are unable to actually do the things yourself. Knowledge is yours, but application is not.

How this knowledge gets applied in the production of something new is a matter of technique, and technique is the business of the sixth house. The way things get done, both for yourself and for other people's benefit, is all in the sixth. Everything you do on someone else's behalf is there, too. If you have the Sun in the sixth house, you are careful and considerate by nature, much concerned to make the best use of things and to do things in the best way possible. Pride of work and craftsmanship are guiding words to you; any kind of sloppiness is upsetting. You look after yourself, too; health is a sixth-house thing, and the Sun in the sixth sometimes makes you something of a hypochondriac.

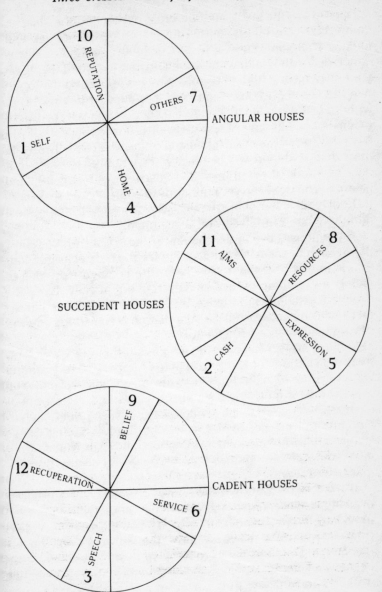

Opposed to the sixth, and therefore opposed to the ideas of doing things for others, mastering the proper technique, and looking after your physical health, is the twelfth house. This is concerned with withdrawing yourself from the world, being on your own, having time to think. Energy is applied to the job in hand in the sixth house, and here it is allowed to grow again without being applied to anything. Recuperation is a good word to remember. All forms of rest are twelfth-house concepts. If you have the Sun in the twelfth house you are an essentially private individual, and there will be times when you need to be on your own to think about things and recover your strength and balance. You will keep your opinions to yourself, and share very little of your emotional troubles with anyone. Yours is most definitely not a life lived out in the open.

These houses live in the shadow of the houses which follow them. Each of them is a preparation for the next phase. If your Sun is in any of these houses, your life is much more one of giving away than of accumulation. You already have the experience and the knowledge, and you will be trying to hand it on before you go, so to speak. Acquisition is something you will never manage on a permanent basis.

If these houses have Cardinal signs on them in your chart, then preparation for things to come is important to you, and you think in straight lines towards a recognized goal. You will have firm and rather simplistic views and beliefs about matters which are not usually described in such terms, such as morality and politics, and you will be used to saying things simply and with meaning. Deception and half-truths, even mild exaggeration, confuse you, because you do not think in that sort of way.

If fixed signs occupy these houses in your horoscope, your thinking is conservative, and your mind, though rich and varied in its imagination, is not truly original. You like to collect ideas from elsewhere and tell yourself that they are your own. You rely on changing circumstances to bring you variety, and your own beliefs and opinions stay fixed to anchor you in a changing world; unfortunately, this can mean a refusal to take in new deas, shown in your behaviour as a rather appealing old-ashionedness.

Having mutable signs on these houses in your horoscope shows a flexible imagination, though often not a very practical one. Speech and ideas flow freely from you, and you are quick to adapt your ideas to suit the occasion, performing complete changes of viewpoint without effort if required. You seem to have grasped the instinctive truth that mental images and words are not real, and can be changed or erased at will; you are far less inhibited in their use than the other two groups, who regard words as something at least as heavy as cement, and nearly as difficult to dissolve. Periods in the public eye and periods of isolation are of equal value to you; you can use them each for their best purpose, and have no dislike of either. This great flexibility of mind does mean, though, that you lack seriousness of approach at times, and have a happy-go-lucky view of the future, and of things spiritual, which may lead to eventual disappointments and regrets.

Houses are important in a horoscope. The twelve sectors of the sky correspond to the twelve signs of the zodiac, the difference being that the zodiac is a product of the Sun's annual revolution, and the houses are a product (via the Ascendant) of the Earth's daily revolution. They bring the symbolism down one level from the sky to the individual, and they answer the questions which arise when people of the same Sun sign have different lives and different preferences. The house in which the Sun falls, and the qualities of the signs in the houses, show each person's approach to those areas of his life, and the one which will be the most important to him.

Part 4

Scorpio Trivia

7. Tastes and Preferences

Clothes

Scorpios are usually very noticeable for their style of dress. It is often very luxurious, and sometimes a little theatrical in the case of women; in all cases, though, it gives the impression of power.

A Scorpio's favourite colours are red and black. Red shows the energy of Mars, and the intensity of energy which the Scorpio brings to every aspect of his life, while black shows the power of restraint and denial with which he masters his emotional forces. Red and black are also the colours of blood and death, of course; in other words, they are the colours of our most deep and vital fears and feelings. Scorpios are well-versed in these; they conduct every moment of their life at that level of intensity, and the colours they choose reflect this. To the onlooker, though, the combination of such strong colours and the powerful, almost sexual nature of Scorpionic energy is a little hard to take all at once; it certainly can't be ignored.

Restraint is usually seen as a good thing in a man's way of dressing, and so male Scorpios are usually to be found in business suits during the day. They are noticeable because the quality of the cloth is usually higher than one might expect, and the colour is just a shade darker. In a society where most businessmen look the same, the Scorpio is concerned to show that he has something deeper, more mysterious, and of a different quality.

In their spare time, Scorpio men like to show strength and purpose through their clothes. The colours are still on the dark side, and the shapes a little formal by comparison with some other signs, but the fabrics are much more varied. There is almost never any decoration, nor is anything worn too loose; such things show a changeable and a lightweight mind, and the Scorpio won't allow that.

Both sexes are widely supposed to be fond of leather. It is true to a certain extent, though to be accurate it is Capricorn's material; a little thought, though, will help you see why Scorpios should find it so attractive. It is an extra skin; it is hard, impenetrable, and protects the wearer. Scorpios like the idea of protecting themselves from the outside world. It is also a sensual material, because of its animal qualities, and its smell. This causes an emotional, and sometimes sexual response, in both the onlooker and the wearer, and it is this kind of energy with which the Scorpio is most familiar. If his clothes produce this kind of emotion by themselves, then he is bound to like them, isn't he? Besides, leather is a power symbol because of its relative expense, which is another Scorpio plus point; and last but not least it is often black.

Scorpio women often dress in dramatic styles to express, and receive, that strong emotional response they need so much. They are equally at home in both the 'little black dress' or something far more dazzling, but they will never wear anything which has weak colours or a soft outline. Romantic frills and pastels can't communicate the power of a Scorpio, so she will choose something with direct and uninterrupted lines, and clear colours. They like showing and hiding the body at the same time; whenever tight or revealing clothes are fashionable, Scorpio women are pleased. Loose or floaty fashions are generally ignored—Scorpios know what they have to do to express that Martian energy, and will do it regardless of fashion if necessary.

Food and Furnishings

Scorpio food is easy to understand—it needs to be strong and powerful in flavour, and provoke a response. If it is in some way associated with sex, so much the better. That gives quite a range to choose from. Highly spiced or hot food (such as chili) is usually to their taste, because of the Martian heat of the peppers and spices, and all kinds of seafood go down well because of the Water sign association. Scorpio is the fixed Water sign, and so prefers the larger sea animals; how about crab or lobster instead of prawns? Most shellfish are supposed to be aphrodisiacs, and even if they are not, Scorpios enjoy the emotion generated by the idea. Failing that, he likes rich flavours associated with power and position, so all red meats and classic wines will attract him too. Like their other Water sign friends Pisces, Scorpios enjoy alcohol; you may need brandy in this instance, to adequately express the heat of Mars.

Scorpio homes are places of the senses. Everything in them is calculated to produce a strong emotional reaction. This means that the decoration will be in strong colours, and the furniture will be chosen for effect rather than because it is cheap and cheerful, or because it has nostalgic associations. It sounds a bit obvious to say that there will be a leather sofa, but it is surprising how many Scorpios do like leather furniture. Often considerable time and money have been lavished on the bedroom and bathroom; they are private places for sensual activities, and the Scorpio values the time he spends in them.

Hobbies

Scorpios don't have a great deal of spare time—at least, not time where they lie about not doing a great deal. Mars keeps them active the whole time, and the sort of sporting activities which appeal to them are the ones where self-control is needed in dangerous circumstances. Motorized sports are a good example, especially motorcycling; so are things like potholing and mountaineering, where concentration and self-discipline are part of the adventure. Being a Water sign, they like active water sports, and particularly *under*water sports, which offer the right combination of physical activity, exploration, and risk.

When they can't go out, they read. Anything which offers the ideas of secrecy and finding out appeals, so favourite novels are usually spy stories or whodunnits.

8. Scorpio Luck

Being lucky isn't a matter of pure luck. It can be engineered. What happens when you are lucky is that a number of correspondences are made between circumstances, people, and even material items, which eventually enable planetary energies to flow quickly and effectively to act with full force in a particular way. If you are part of that chain, or your intentions lie in the same direction as the planetary flow, then you say that things are going your way, or that you are lucky. All you have to do to maximize this tendency is to make sure you are aligned to the flow of energies from the planets whenever you want things to work your way.

It is regular astrological practice to try to reinforce your own position in these things, by attracting energies which are already strongly represented in you. For a Scorpio, this means Mars, of course, and therefore any 'lucky' number, colour, or whatever for a Scorpio is simply going to be one which corresponds symbolically to the attributes of Mars.

Mars' colour is red, and Scorpio's colour is black; therefore a Scorpio person's lucky colours are red and black, because by wearing them or aligning himself to them, for example by betting on a horse whose jockey's silks are red or black, or supporting a sporting team whose colours include red, he aligns himself to the energies of Mars, and thereby recharges the solar energies that are already in him.

A Scorpio's preferred gemstone is jasper; bloodstone is often quoted for Mars too. Gemstones are seen as being able to concentrate or focus magical energies, and the colour of the stone shows its propensity to the energies of a particular planet. There are other stones quoted for the sign, such as topaz and malachite, but in most cases it is the colour which is the key.

Because Scorpio is the eighth sign, your lucky number is 8; all combinations of numbers which add up to 8 by reduction work the same way, so you have a range to choose from. Reducing a number is done by adding its digits until you can go no further. As an example, take 476, $4 + 7 + 6 = 17$, and then $1 + 7 = 8$. There you are—476 is a lucky number for you, so to buy a car with those digits in its registration plate would make it a car which, while you had it, you were very fond of, and which served you well.

Mars has its own number, which is 5. The same rules apply as they did with 8. Mars also has its own day, Tuesday (mardi in French, which is Mars' day), and Scorpio has a direction with which it is associated, the South. If you have something important to do, and you manage to put it into action early in the morning of Tuesday 5 August (month number 8, remember), then you will have made sure that you will get the result best suited to you, by aligning yourself to your own planet and helping its energies flow through you and your activity unimpeded.

Mars also has a metal associated with it, and in the Middle Ages people wore jewellery made of their planetary metals for luck, or self-alignment and emphasis, whichever way you want to describe it. In the case of Scorpio and Mars, that metal is iron, which is a pity in some ways, because personal ornaments made of iron have never been as popular as silver and gold. Perhaps your car is steel jewellery: is it red or black?

There are plants and herbs for each planet, and foods too. Among the Martian plants are basil, coriander, garlic, ginger– and tobacco!

There is almost no end to the list of correspondences between the planets and everyday items, and many more can be made if you have a good imagination. They are lucky for Scorpios if you know what makes them so, and if you believe them to be so; the essence of the process lies in linking yourself and the object of your intent with some identifiable token of your own planet, such as its colour or number, and strengthening yourself thereby. The stronger you are, then the more frequently you will be able to achieve the result you want—and that's all that luck is, isn't it?

A Final Word

By the time you reach here, you will have learnt a great deal more about yourself. At least, I hope you have.

You will probably have noticed that I appear to have contradicted myself in some parts of the book, and repeated myself in others, and there are reasons for this. It is quite likely that I have said that your Sun position makes you one way, while your Ascendant makes you the opposite. There is nothing strange about this; nobody is consistent, the same the whole way through—everybody has contradictory sides to their character, and knowing some more about your Sun sign and your Ascendant will help you to label and define those contradictory elements. It won't do anything about dealing with them, though—that's your job, and always has been. The only person who can live your horoscope is you. Astrology won't make your problems disappear, and it never has been able to; it simply defines the problems more clearly, and enables you to look for answers.

Where I have repeated myself it is either to make the point for the benefit of the person who is only going to read that section of the book, or because you have a double helping of the energy of your sign, as in the instance of the Sun and Ascendant in the same sign.

I hope you found the relationships section useful; you may well find that the Sun-to-Ascendant comparison is just as useful in showing you how you fit in with your partner as the usual Sun-to-Sun practice.

Where do you go from here? If you want to learn more about astrology, and see how all of the planets fit into the picture of the sky as it was at your birth, then you must either consult an astrologer or learn how to do it for yourself. There is quite a lot of astrology around these days; evening classes are not too hard to find and there are groups of enthusiasts up and down the country. There are also plenty of books which will show you how to draw up and interpret your own horoscope.

One thing about doing it yourself, which is an annoyance unless you are aware of it in advance: to calculate your horoscope properly you will need to know where the planets were in the sky when you were born, and you usually have to buy this data separately in a book called an ephemeris. The reason that astrology books don't have this data in them is that to include enough for everybody who is likely to buy the book would make the book as big as a phone directory, and look like a giant book of log tables, which is a bit off-putting. You can buy ephemerides (the plural) for any single year, such as the one of your birth. You can also buy omnibus versions for the whole century.

So, you will need two books, not one: an ephemeris, and a book to help you draw up and interpret your horoscope. It's much less annoying when you *know* you're going to need two books.

After that, there are lots of books on the more advanced techniques in the Astrology Handbook series, also from the Aquarian Press. Good though the books are, there is no substitute for being taught by an astrologer, and no substitute at all for practice. What we are trying to do here is provide a vocabulary of symbols taken from the sky so that you and your imagination can make sense of the world you live in; the essential element is your imagination, and you provide that.

Astrology works perfectly well at Sun sign level, and it works perfectly well at deeper levels as well; you can do it with what you want. I hope that, whatever you do with it, it is both instructive and satisfying to you—and fun, too.

SUNS AND LOVERS

The Astrology of Sexual Relationships

Penny Thornton. It doesn't seem to matter how experienced –
or inexperienced – you are, when it comes to love and romance
there just *isn't* a fool proof formula. . . but this book does its best
to provide one! THE definitive astrological guide to sexual
relationships, this book is based upon the accumulated wisdom,
and observations of centuries of dedicated astrologers. Reveals:

- In-depth analysis of astrological types
- Male and female profiles for each star sign
- Zodiacal attitudes to intimate relationships
- Most compatible – and incompatible – partners

Each general star sign analysis is concluded with amazingly
frank reflections, often based upon personal interviews, with
many famous personalities including: Bob Champion; Suzi
Quatro; Colin Wilson; Jeremy Irons; HRH The Princess Anne;
HRH The Duke of York; Martin Shaw; Barbara Cartland; Twiggy
and many more. Written in an easy-to-read style, and packed
with illuminating and fascinating tit-bits, this book is compulsive
reading for anyone likely to have *any sort* of encounter with the
opposite sex!